THE
USEFUL
LIE

THE
USEFUL
LIE

William L. Playfair, M.D.
with George Bryson

CROSSWAY BOOKS • WHEATON, ILLINOIS
A DIVISION OF GOOD NEWS PUBLISHERS

The Useful Lie

Copyright © 1991 by William L. Playfair, M.D.

Published by Crossway Books, a division of
Good News Publishers, 1300 Crescent Street,
Wheaton, Illinois 60187.

First printing, 1991

Printed in the United States of America

Unless otherwise noted, all Bible quotations are taken from
Holy Bible: New International Version, copyright © 1978 by
the New York International Bible Society. Used by permission
of Zondervan Bible Publishers.

Library of Congress Cataloging-in-Publication Data
Playfair, William L.,
    The useful lie/ William L. Playfair with George Bryson.
        p.   cm.
Includes bibliographical references.
        1. Alchoholism—Religious aspects—Christianity. 2. Drug
abuse—Religious aspects—Christianity. 3. Co-dependence
(Psychology)—Religious aspects—Christianity. 4. Twelve step
programs—Religious aspects—Christianity. 5. Temperance. 6. Sin.
I. Bryson, George. II. Title.
BV4596.A48P42 1991   261.8'3229—dc20   91-21797
ISBN 0-89107-637-9

99		98		97		96		95		94		93		92		91
15	14	13	12	11	10	9	8	7	6	5	4	3	2	

This book is dedicated to
Paul "Skip" Schilperoort
Mentor and Fellow Pilgrim

Contents

PART 3

Acknowledgments

I am deeply indebted to Herbert Fingarette and Stanton Peele whose writings sparked my desire to write this book. Although they will not necessarily agree with my Biblical approach to the problem, no one writes about addiction mythology with greater clarity than do these two scholars. Also Pastor R. Scott Clark shared invaluable information and insights with me.

Many others have supplied encouragement and offered suggestions regarding the manuscript, among them: Steve Austin of the Santa Fe Christian School Board, Carolyn and Pastor Jim Bucher, Alice Thuma, Skip Schilperoort, Dr. Andrew Peterson of the Christian Counseling and Educational Foundation/West, Bob and Mary Jane Mitchell, John Van Diest, and Tom Compton.

Jay Adams and John Sowell supplied valuable encouragement and advice. Jay added superb assistance on the manuscript itself.

A special thanks goes to three people. In addition to supplying constant encouragement, Dr. Alwyn Zoutendyk introduced the manuscript to Muriel and Jan Dennis, who "took it and ran with it," for which I will be eternally grateful.

Most of all, I am grateful for the support and encouragement of Kathryn and Emmy, who endured the stresses that accompany the writing of a book.

Janet's Story

Janet, the wife of a church elder, was involved in the children's ministry of her fellowship. She was not much for socializing and always seemed to be a little uncomfortable in a gathering of adults. Her pastor suspected something was not right but could not be sure. On several occasions he asked her if something was bothering her that she'd like to talk about. She would insist that she had always been a very private person, and even small groups made her nervous. Every month when the pastor and elders and their wives met for fellowship and prayer, Janet's husband, Dan, would usually have a different excuse for her absence. One month she was "out of town," the next she'd "had a bad headache," and so on. In three years she attended only two of these gatherings and left early in both instances.

Finally Dan's closest friend, Carl, said to him, "I know something is wrong with you and Janet. Please talk to me about it." Dan couldn't wait to get the burden he had been bearing for several years off his chest. Although Janet had made him promise he wouldn't tell, out it poured!

Dan said that Janet had a serious drinking problem. Every night after tucking in the children, she would hit the liquor cabinet. From about nine to twelve, she would drink herself to sleep, and every morning she would wake up with a hangover, feeling guilty and trapped. She never drank during the day. She never drank around the kids. She never drank socially. But every night, she drank. Her life revolved around it. Dan said he had prayed with her, pleaded with her, threatened her, but nothing helped. He did not want to admit what was painfully evident – his wife was an alcoholic. She was, in many ways, a good wife, great with the kids, and serious about her faith in Christ. This, however, was one area of life over which she seemed to have no control.

Carl assured Dan that the situation would be kept confidential. No one in the church need know. However, they would need to get help. He said Janet should be convinced to enter a recovery program of some kind and then join Alcoholics Anonymous.

With the help of a local treatment center covered by Dan's health care insurance, Carl confronted Janet. After a very traumatic period, Janet entered treatment for alcoholism, joined AA, and started attending what AA calls "closed" meetings. Dan attended Al-Anon, a family support group for family members. Their four-teen-year-old daughter went to Al-Ateen, and their three-year-old began going to Al-Atot.

But Janet never did start attending the meetings with the elders and their wives. And Dan stopped com-ing as well. Janet also quit working with the children's ministry. As it turned out, Janet's involvement in AA and Dan's involvement with Al-Anon, not to mention other related activities with the kids, took virtually all their free time.

Further, Janet and Dan reasoned that the church they were attending was a part of the problem, rather than the solution. In treatment, Janet was taught that she had been suffering from a "sickness" called alcoholism. But she was unable to get treatment because she thought it was sin. Janet was very bitter when she remembered all the years she had been hurting, weighed down by guilt and "low self-esteem," all because of some "outdated and unscientific" view of alcohol addiction. Now that she knew the truth, it was very difficult to return to church. She tried on a couple of occasions to enlighten the pastor, but he could not be moved from the conviction that alcohol and drug problems were rooted in sin and that addicts were responsible for that sinful behavior.

Eventually, Janet and Dan decided to break all ties with the church. They told themselves they could do more for God within AA and Al-Anon anyway. They reasoned that many hurting people could not be reached by the church and that with the information they had learned in treatment and through AA, they could make a difference in the lives of other alcoholics and their families. They knew they could not be too specific about God and certainly not about Jesus Christ, but "if they *could* help someone achieve sobriety," well, certainly that would be a step in the right direction, wouldn't it?

Tommy's Story

Tommy was in many ways a typical teenager. He liked sports, cars, and girls. Unfortunately, he also liked to drink on weekends and, on occasion, smoke pot. It was Tommy's senior year, and his grades went from A's and B's to C's and D's. Tommy's Christian parents were understandably concerned. The church they had attended from the time Tommy was a toddler had a program and ministry specifically dealing with the problems of chemical dependency built around a "modified for Christians" version of AA's Twelve Steps.

Tommy's parents went to the director of this program to talk about Tommy's problem. The director explained that Tommy actually had a "common disease" that afflicted a large percentage of the population. As such, his problems were more medical than moral. They needed to understand that Tommy would not and could not help himself. He had had this disease from birth— alcohol and drugs only brought it to the surface. He told them that Tommy would go to his grave with this disease.

There was some hope however. Although his disease was incurable, it was treatable, the director said. They needed to recognize two primary symptoms of the disease—an uncontrollable desire to abuse alcohol or drugs and a state of delusion that causes the alcoholic or drug addict to deny what is obvious to everyone else.

The director recommended that since Tommy was a minor, he should immediately be placed (against his will if need be) into a recovery program for teenagers. When he got out, he could then begin attending the "Christ-centered" Twelve Step program in the church.

Extremely distraught over the situation, Tommy's parents brought in an intervention team from a local recovery center for teens. Although Tommy admitted drinking on weekends (usually two or three beers at parties) and experimenting twice with pot, he denied having a problem. He was sure he could quit on his own. The intervention team, as well as the director of the church program, called this a "symptom of denial" and further proof of his problem.

Tommy was embittered about being labeled an alcoholic and drug addict, but he realized that the longer he resisted treatment and refused to admit he had a chemical dependency problem, the longer he would be incarcerated. Tommy quickly learned to say what the treatment counselors wanted to hear. Thus, using all the right lingo, Tommy became a model patient.

Shortly after Tommy was released, he turned eighteen and left home without even saying good-bye. Knowing the church had put his parents up to incarcerating him in the recovery program, Tommy vowed never to return to church again. He also began drinking much more than before. He reasoned to himself: "If I'm going to be treated like an alcoholic, I might as well act like one."

The church director assured his parents that Tommy's condition (and not their response to that condition) had contributed to his continued and even more serious substance abuse. Something, however, made Tommy's parents think that they may have mishandled the situation. They found little solace in the director's insistence that they had done the right thing.

Jack's Story

J ack was an executive in a major accounting firm. In his business one- and two-martini lunches were rather common. Because Jack was a Christian, he never allowed himself more than one drink per meal, no matter what. But he almost always had one drink, much to the concern of his wife Barbara. Both of her parents were serious substance abusers. Her father was an alcoholic, and her mother was hooked on a variety of prescription drugs. Barbara worried that Jack had become an alcoholic without realizing it.

She attended a series of classes in her adult Sunday school that focused upon the adult children of alcoholics and on what the teacher called "codependents." Barbara became convinced Jack was an alcoholic and she was a codependent. She knew she had always worried too much, and now she knew why. She had become "too loving and too caring" in her relationship with Jack. It was time to start taking care of herself.

Following the advice in several books referred to her by her Sunday school teacher, Barbara decided to join a support group for codependents. She became convinced it was time to confront Jack about his supposed drinking problem. "If he is unwilling to get help or go to

AA," she decided, "I'll leave him. After all, love must be tough!" She was not prepared for the speed with which Jack packed his bags. Within a year he relocated and remarried. Barbara was devastated; it was not supposed to work out that way!

≈ ≈ ≈

In reading these stories you may have asked yourself several important questions.

    1. Now that Janet is sober and dedicated to helping others achieve and maintain sobriety, can we conclude that this story had a happy ending, as far as it goes?

    2. Did Tommy's parents "do the right thing" by placing him in a recovery program?

    3. Does the evidence suggest that Jack was an "alcoholic" waiting to happen?

It was to answer these and similar questions that *The Useful Lie* was written. At the end of this book is a biblical "rewrite" of these same stories, but wait until you finish reading the book to turn there.

Part 1

One
The Mistreatment Industry:

The Church and the World

As a Christian physician, I am concerned about the adverse impact the alcohol and drug addiction recovery industry is having upon the nation and the church. No doubt about it, alcoholism and drug addiction are very serious problems. As a Christian and as a medical doctor, I am deeply disturbed about their awful consequences, especially when these consequences fall upon fellow Christians. The painful truth is that sometimes Christians *do* become addicted to alcohol and/or drugs. Who among us does not have a loved one, friend, or neighbor (either Christian or non-Christian) who struggles with alcohol or drug abuse? The problems seem almost epidemic. Of all people, Christians should thus rise to the challenge posed by alcoholism and drug addiction, offering mercy and hope to those affected.

We who are ambassadors for Christ do not have the luxury of sitting on the sidelines as neutral observers. After all, Christ died for alcoholics and drug addicts. If the expression "Christ is the answer" means more to us than a slogan on a bumper sticker, or if there is any social significance to our Lord's command to be "salt and light," we will want to do what we can to help.

We must, however, be discerning in how we help. Not every well-intended effort is worthy of our support. Some attempts to solve grave societal problems actually exacerbate them. Some cures are worse than the disease. Take Marxism, for example. Governments apply its principles to an economy intending that the poor should "share in the wealth" with the rich. Instead, everyone is impoverished. Rather than helping the poor *up* the economic ladder, Marxism brings the wealthy and middle classes *down* to the lowest economic level. With the exception of a few power brokers, no one is helped, and practically everyone is hurt.

So it is with the addiction recovery industry. I have no doubts about the sincere intentions and well-meaning efforts of many who work in this area. Most really do want to help the alcoholic and the drug addict and may sacrifice a great deal to do so. As it turns out, however, their efforts are seriously misguided.

Surprising as this may seem, the recovery industry, as a whole, is not helping, but actually *hurting* the people it is trying to help. Three recently published books document the largely negative impact of recovery programs. In 1988, Professor Herbert Fingarette dropped a bombshell with his book *Heavy Drinking: The Myth of Alcoholism as a Disease.* Shortly after, social-clinical psychologist Stanton Peele published *Diseasing of America: Addiction Treatment Out of Control.* Finally, renowned clinical psychologist Stan Katz and journalist Aimee E. Liu published *The Codependency Conspiracy: How to Break the Recovery Habit and Take Charge of Your Life.* All three books consider the notion that alcoholism and drug addiction are "diseases" requiring medical treatment to be unscientific and counterproductive. According to these authors, and virtually all studies from medical science research, the disease concept is at best spurious.

My concern is that the disease concept so central to the recovery industry has not only taken popular culture by storm, but has found its way into the church of Jesus Christ as well. Although science debunks it and Scripture contradicts it, this view now thoroughly dominates many Christian programs dealing with addictive behaviors. This is true both in terms of what Christians are attempting to do inside and outside the church community. The wholesale acceptance of the disease concept has thus rendered the church as ineffective as the recovery industry. To make matters worse, the disease concept is now being applied to innumerable other problems ranging from overeating and overworking to excessive permissiveness.

As a result, we live in a time when Christian counselors view stealing, lying, infidelity, undereating, hot-headedness, *ad infinitum,* as diseases that must be treated. Perpetrators of crimes are now treated as patients instead of punished as criminals. It is a tragedy that non-Christian programs designed to reach "alcoholics," "drug addicts," the parents, children, and friends of "alcoholics and drug addicts," the unfaithful, the spouse or children of the unfaithful, the angry, the children of the angry, etc., have promoted this diseasing of America. But it is far worse to think that the church, "pillar of the truth," could be guilty of the diseasing of Christianity.

The recovery industry is not only *not* a solution to the problem of addictive behaviors—it is part of the problem. It is a self-perpetuating system propped up by wishful thinking and useful lies. By turning to the recovery industry for answers, the church has turned *away* from real solutions. That is the bad news. The good news is that it is not too late to turn back to the one true God, to the real answer to the problem found in His one and only Son.

To say Jesus Christ is the answer to addictive behavior is not simplistic—as some Christians claim. Rather, it is the most profound of all truths. By misdiagnosing various addictions as medical problems, the recovery industry mistreats people. What does this say about the many church-related programs that incorporate the views and practices of the recovery industry? Let us turn to God's wisdom as we consider the diseasing of Christianity in light of both Scripture and science.

Two

The Diseasing of Christianity:

Sin vs. Sickness

Not too long ago Christians and non-Christians alike believed that what is today referred to as "alcoholism" or "drug addiction"—"chemical dependency"—was the consequence of the regular and long-term "sinful" use of alcohol and drugs.

In the case of alcohol, it simply meant excessive drinking. Most people thought heavy drinking on a regular, long-term basis led to addictive drinking; it was just a matter of drinking too much too often. While psychological dependency might come before physiological addiction, it was "immoderate drinking" over the long run, according to this view, that resulted in "alcoholism" as such.

Likewise, people considered that the nonmedicinal and recreational use of drugs (i.e., getting high, loaded, stoned, etc.) would eventually lead to drug addiction. (Occasionally, someone such as an amputee might become addicted to morphine, but this is the exception, not the rule. While this may be a problem, it is not the kind of problem with which this book is concerned.)

According to this traditional view, most drug users became addicts by misusing or abusing drugs. It is that simple. Drug addicts were therefore considered immoral, because it was immorality, or the sinful use of drugs, that brought about addiction. (This straightforward view of chemical dependency is thoroughly rejected by the contemporary American addiction recovery industry.) It favors the "sickness" view over the "sin" view. Amazingly, this wholesale reversal was due in large part to the efforts of a single organization. As Ernest Kurtz in *Not-God: A History of Alcoholics Anonymous* says:

> The widespread diffusion of the "disease concept of alcoholism" was largely due to Alcoholics Anonymous.[1]

More important, affirming alcoholism (or drug addiction—the purview of AA spinoff groups such as Narcotics Anonymous) as a medical disease denies moral depravity or culpability. Al-Anon speaks for virtually the entire recovery industry when it says:

> After centuries of treating alcoholism as a moral weakness, most present-day medical opinion considers alcoholism a disease which, like diabetes, can be arrested, but not cured. Many of the clergy, too, now accept alcoholism as sickness, and not sin.[2]

In the next chapter we shall consider the scientific merits, or lack thereof, of the disease concept of chemical dependency. For now, I only wish to point out that AA clearly states that chemical dependency does not stem from both sin and sickness. I mention this because many Christians have tried to reconcile these two contradictory views. But you cannot have it both ways. If addiction is the result of sin, the alcoholic or drug addict is morally culpable. If chemical dependency is the consequence of sickness, he is no more responsible for his condition than a diabetic. Or rather, we should say he is responsible in the same way. In this view there is no real guilt.

While America's addictions recovery industry got its disease concept largely from AA, the organization got it from life-long friend and supporter of AA, Dr. William Silkworth. His contribution to this concept will be considered elsewhere.

What is important to recognize at this time is that when AA and the recovery industry refer to the *disease* of chemical dependency, they are not using this word metaphorically or in some extended sense. That is, they are not saying alcoholism and drug addiction are *like* a medical disease. They are saying they *are* medical diseases. As Ernest Kurtz says of Bill W., co-founder of AA:

> . . . his usual terms "illness" or "malady" as well as his frequent comparison of alcoholism to "heart disease"

bear witness to his acceptance of Silkworth's medical ideas.[3]

It is this medical view, in slightly updated and modified form, that dominates the thinking of today's addictions recovery industry. The earlier traditional view is called the *moral model*. The recovery industry's view is called the *medical model*. While the moral model recognizes that medical problems often result from or are complicated by substance abuse, it sees addiction as primarily a moral problem with a moral solution. On the other hand, the medical model sees addiction as primarily a medical problem with a medical solution.

Since the primary concern of this book is to counter the church's acceptance of the unscriptural disease concept of alcoholism and drug addiction, I will use the term moral model to refer to the Biblical view.

Moral Model	Medical Model
The addict became addicted primarily as the result of *immoral behavior*.	The addict became addicted primarily as the result of *amoral biology*.
The addict is first and foremost and foremost *guilty* of *sin*.	The addict is first the *victim* of *sickness*.
The addict is *spiritually* and *morally depraved*.	The addict is *psychologically* and *physically diseased*.

While the terms "alcoholic" and "drug addict" do not appear in Scripture, God's Word does speak clearly to the issue of alcohol abuse. It calls those addicted to alcohol drunkards (Deuteronomy 21:20; Proverbs 23:21; 26:9; Isaiah 24:20; 1 Corinthians 5:11). Certainly, the alcoholic or drug addict is a person *controlled* by his or her habit. Yet the Christian is to be controlled by the Holy Spirit. The Apostle Paul says, "I *will* not be brought under the power of any[thing]" (1 Corinthians 6:12 KJV). Note his use of the word *will*. We have a choice in such matters.

To be "under the power" includes not only excessive drinking or nonmedicinal drug use as a way of life, but also occasional intoxication. If one is not guilty of the former, he will not succumb to the latter. Such dissipation is strictly forbidden by God and hence is sin (Ephesians 5:18). The unrighteous person is listed right alongside other sinners—"fornicators," "idolaters," "adulterers," "homosexuals," "*drunkards*" (1 Corinthians 6:9-10). What is an alcoholic but a drunkard, and for all practical purposes, drug abusers are to drugs what drunkards are to alcohol. Substance misuse or abuse has brought these people "under the power." Such an uncontrolled lifestyle is called unrighteousness (sin). According to John, "If we confess our *sins*, he [Christ] is faithful and just and will forgive us our sins and purify us from all *unrighteousness*" (1 John 1:9).

There is no escaping this basic fact—the Bible considers addictive behaviors to be the result of willful acts of iniquity. Paul says: "The acts of the sinful nature are obvious: . . . *drunkenness* . . . " (Galatians 5 :19).

(The Bible does not recognize a *can* or *cannot* category of user. One either does or does not, will or will not, abuse alcohol or drugs.) Of course, sins such as alcohol and drug abuse are capable of bringing about enslavement. But then all sinning is to a large extent a form of slavery. Jesus said, " . . . everyone who sins is a slave to sin" (John 8:34).

If one has abused alcohol or drugs to the point of becoming addicted, it is past time he or she confessed that as *sin*. I say past time because it is the sin of abuse, compounded over a long period of time, that leads to the sinful condition of addiction.

The spiritual and practical importance of recognizing addiction to alcohol or drugs for what it is—sin—will become even more clear as we progress. For now, it is enough to say, to deny that addiction is sin is to forfeit forgiveness (Unforgiven sin, in whatever form it manifests itself, breaks and blocks fellowship with God.) As Isaiah tells it, it is sin that separates a person from God (Isaiah 59:2). Confessing sin and receiving forgiveness restores fellowship with God, the first genuine step toward freedom from addictions. After the first step, some may need counseling to help them understand and deal with issues from the past that hinder their recovery.

To accept the medical model of addiction is, at best, counterproductive and, at worst, destructive. "Why then," one may ask, "if Scripture is so clear about the real cause of substance abuse (i.e., sin) are so many Christians siding with the recovery industry?" No doubt, there are many reasons why believers fail to see alcoholism and drug addiction for what they really are. Perhaps, most important, is the fact that many Christians, like non-Christians, are impressed by what purports to be science. All too often though, what passes for science turns out to be little more than pseudoscience. This is true in the case of the "sickness" view of substance abuse.

Christians also deny the sinfulness of addictive behavior because they find it difficult to believe that any believer can really be all that bad. After all, they reason, to see someone as a willful alcoholic or drug addict could very well call into question that person's salvation. This conclusion is quite unfortunate.

Since Scripture says Christians ought not to use alcohol or drugs sinfully, it must be possible for them to do so. The same can be said for every other sin. Addiction is uncharacteristic of the way Christians *ought* to behave, but that does not mean Christians are incapable of becoming addicts. For whatever reason, "redefining" sin ultimately only denies it, and to deny it more than likely leads one to be overcome by it.

Every Christian should heed the words of Paul, "For you were once darkness, but now you are light in the Lord. Live as children of light (for the fruit of the light consists in all goodness, righteousness and truth) and find out what pleases the Lord. Have nothing to do with the fruitless deeds of darkness, but rather expose them

. . . everything exposed by the light becomes visible, for it is light that makes everything visible" (Ephesians 5: 8-14).

The light of God's Word illuminates our hearts and minds, shows us our sinful behavior, and enables us to see sin for what it really is. Let us say with King David, "Your word is a lamp to my feet and a light for my path" (Psalm 119:105).

If you are addicted to alcohol or drugs, Scripture teaches that you can confess your sin, be forgiven, overcome your sin, and be restored to fellowship with God. If you reject God's Word and deny your sin, you will forfeit the forgiveness and restoration that could be yours. The choice is yours. But be sure of one thing: if you are truly a child of God, He will discipline you (Hebrews 12:8) and eventually bring you to repentance and confession. Why go through unnecessary agony and misery when God can help you end your addiction now?

Three

The Open Secret:

Science vs. Sickness

like evolution scientist have chosen to accept an unprovable theory as fact because it is either pragmatic and/or convenient

Christians should reject the view of alcoholism and drug addiction as illnesses, (if for no other reason,) because this view contradicts God's Word. However, there is another very good reason why we should not accept the medical model of addiction. This model is as much *unscientific* as it is *unscriptural*. Thus, the recovery industry is seriously out of step with the very science upon which its views and practices are supposedly based.

The classic disease concept of addiction states that alcoholics and drug addicts have a disease that is biological in etiology. That is, they were born with this disease. The disease becomes manifest upon exposure to alcohol or mood-altering drugs. After such exposure, the victim progresses to using increasingly greater amounts of the chemical, becoming tolerant to its effects, losing control over its use, abrogating all power of choice as he develops an insatiable craving for it. The victim eventually "bottoms out" and dies unless he receives treatment. As the result of treatment he must be converted to a life-long program of total abstinence from alcohol and all mood-altering substances. He must also regularly attend group meetings for support to prevent falling back into the disease pattern.

For some with this disease, the road from use to abuse is very gradual and perhaps even intermittent. For others, immoderate or irresponsible use of chemicals may follow immediately after the first exposure to them. Thus, some people are affected more dramatically than others. However, if someone who has the disease uses such chemicals, he or she will inevitably become addicted to them.

And yet, despite the universal acceptance of this medical model of chemical dependency, one would be hard-pressed to find a medical science researcher who accepts it. Fingarette, author of *Heavy Drinking: The Myth of Alcoholism as a Disease,* calls this an "open secret."[1] The results of research published in scientific journals strongly contradict popular beliefs. Nevertheless, the general public, and to a great degree the Christian community, reflect the ignorance prevalent in much of the recovery industry itself. That is because "many counselors and professionals working in treatment centers—remain in the dark, still holding, and encouraged to hold, beliefs that are forty years out of date."[2]

Were one to review the history of modern medicine, one would see three distinct generations of diseases. The first generation includes those disorders known by their physical manifestations, such as pneumonia, cancer, chicken pox. Some part of the body malfunctions, accompanied by obvious physical symptoms. The treatment for these diseases follows specific medical practices—perform an operation, administer medication, assess the results of treatment, and so on.

The second generation of diseases, comprised of emotional disorders that are manifested by the feelings and thoughts of the sufferer, can only be recognized by asking the sufferer about his thoughts, feelings, etc. This category includes such disorders as depression, phobias, schizophrenia, and manic-depression. Interestingly, some believe that many of these second-generation diseases will ultimately, with greater scientific knowledge and particularly with the development of molecular biology, be reclassified as belonging to the first generation. That is, they will be treated with pills or surgery. Many would now place schizophrenia and manic-depressive illness into the first generation because often they are effectively treated with medication.

The third generation of "diseases" encompasses addictions. Their symptoms are not disordered bodily function or disordered thinking, but rather disordered or abnormal *behavior*. Thus, we include alcoholism, drug addiction, compulsive gambling, pedophilia, compulsive bank robbery—all the things society used to call sin or immoral conduct. Please notice the distinct attempt by those in the addictions recovery industry to relate these third-generation "diseases" to amoral biology by placing them in the first generation of diseases. That is to say, addicts are *born* that way. According to this view, they are victims of their genetic make-up.[3]

To recapitulate, one who suffers with a third-generation "disease":

● has lost all control of his involvement in the activity.

● must attend group support meetings and totally abstain from the behavior for the rest of his life.

● was born that way and will die with the disease.

● will easily become addicted to mood-altering drugs or activities similar to his drug or activity of choice.

● denies he has the disease until confronted by disease experts or fellow sufferers.

Let us now look at these in greater detail.

LOSS OF CONTROL

The classic disease concept claims that the "untreated" alcoholic cannot limit his drinking, despite the problems drinking causes. The reason according to the recovery industry is simple: he is biologically incapable of controlling it. This loss of self-control is thought to be a prominent and even primary symptom of the "disease of alcoholism." It is manifested in two ways:

1. The untreated alcoholic is unable to resist taking that first drink after abstaining for a time; i.e., he has an uncontrollable "craving" to drink.

Anderson Spickard, author of *Dying for a Drink,* states it as follows:

> While the alcohol abuser chooses to get drunk, the alcoholic drinks involuntarily. His will power is in service to his addiction and he cannot resist his craving for alcohol. Telling an alcohol addict to shape up and stop drinking is like telling a man who jumps out of a nine-story building to fall only three floors.[4]

The book, *Alcoholics Anonymous,* as well as the recovery industry in general, claims that the alcoholic has lost the power of choice in drinking, that he has no defense against taking the first drink. Part of the goal of AA-type treatment is teaching alcoholics how to overcome the craving for that first drink. (Most of what AA and the recovery industry say about the alcoholic they believe also applies to his drug-abusing counterpart.)

2. The alcoholic (treated or untreated) who has had that first drink is unable to keep from drinking more; hence the AA slogan, "One drink away from a drunk."

The problem of the concept of *craving* is that any attempt to define or characterize it leads inexorably into a tautology. Fingarette explains:

> Whenever an alcoholic drinks in a grossly excessive manner, one can say it is an instance of loss of control caused by craving. But whenever an alcoholic doesn't drink or drinks moderately, one can only say there was

on that occasion no craving. Since there is no independent way of deciding whether craving is or isn't present, the word becomes a synonym for—not an explanation of—excessive drinking.[5]

The claim that alcoholics experience at times an intense desire exceeding their power to resist could just as correctly be applied to a person who indulges in cookies and ice cream. *Craving* is a term that could logically be used to explain why anybody does anything; the word is essentially meaningless. However, this is not to deny that alcoholics have a strong desire for alcohol that they find very difficult to resist.

The recovery industry says that the alcoholic's loss of ability to control or limit his drinking is triggered by that first drink. But if this loss of control occurs only after the first drink, why would abstinence be a major problem? Furthermore, we have all seen people known to be heavy drinkers who are able to stop after one or two drinks. Some say that loss of control is an intermittent phenomenon; that is, sometimes loss of control is a problem for the alcoholic and sometimes it is not. This response so dilutes the concept as to render it useless.

Furthermore, recovery industry disease folklore maintains that even a single taste of alcohol, for instance, in a dessert or cough syrup, will set off an uncontrollable reaction that compels the alcoholic to drink excessively.[6] This concept has been disproven by *every* experiment designed to test it.[7] Scientific analysis has demonstrated that those "alcoholics" who drink the most of a beverage are those who believe that it contains alcohol even when none is present. Furthermore, those alcoholics who believe that their beverage contains no alcohol, even when it does, drink moderately and normally. Therefore the *belief* of the alcoholic is what really matters, rather than the actual alcohol content of his beverage. In fact, innumerable studies have demonstrated that, rather than not being able to control their drinking, alcoholics shoot for a desired level of consciousness, a desired "feelings level" when they drink. That they "overshoot" this "feelings level"—in other words, drink too much—is characteristic of all intoxicants. Just as the relationship of blood alcohol content to the amount of alcohol imbibed is modified by a number of variables, such as amount of food recently ingested, so the relationship of blood alcohol content to resultant mood and feelings is modified by variables (the drinker's expectations, motivations, etc.). This means that alcoholics are no different from other human beings in seeking feelings and mood changes.

In fact, one of the cultural factors most clearly associated with increasing the prevalence of alcoholism is the general acceptance of "alcoholism-as-a-disease." Native Americans, for example, imbue alcohol with enormous power and take it as a "given" that they cannot drink it in a controlled manner. Various American ethnic and cultural groups with low rates of alcoholism, such as the Jewish and Chinese communities, do not accept "loss of control" as an excuse for drunkenness. These cultures assume that their members ought to control their alcohol intake and are fully able to do just that. Thus it appears that to tell people that they are "powerless" over their alcohol consumption is to utter a self-fulfilling prophecy.

TOTAL ABSTINENCE AS TREATMENT

How can we effectively measure the results of dependency treatment? Is total abstinence the only acceptable goal, or ought the goal to be moderation? Virtually all studies have shown that most alcoholics *do* drink again after disease-based treatment programs and that some can sustain moderate levels of drinking for varying amounts of time. Is total abstinence the only desirable goal?

Although the rigidly held belief that the addicted drinker must totally abstain has been thoroughly contradicted by a growing body of scientific literature, most "alcoholism workers" fear that "controlled" drinking in the short term will inexorably lead to uncontrolled drinking in the long term. Some say that allowing controlled drinking is "dangerous and irresponsible."[8] Others have gone so far as to call for the suppression of any scientific studies that indicate the possibility of controlled drinking by a previously addicted drinker.

In the United Kingdom, 75 percent of clinics offer controlled drinking as an alternative.[9] However, our preoccupation with the disease concept in the United States has precluded the development of controlled-drinking programs. Hence, long-term prospective studies of controlled drinking here are lacking. And certainly, "controlled drinking" must be defined. Can one rightly claim to be a controlled drinker if he limits himself to a fifth of hard liquor daily or to no more than three bottles of wine at one sitting?

The controversy over controlled drinking began in 1962 when researcher D. L. Davies[10] noticed reports suggesting that some diagnosed alcoholics successfully maintained a practice of controlled drinking. He was strongly criticized in the press as well as in scientific journals, including the one in which he published his article. But then in 1972, the renowned mental health research team, Mark and Linda Sobell, published the results of their successful program for controlled drinking.[11] In 1976 the highly regarded Rand Report added its confirmation.[12] The National Council on Alcoholism, among others, criticized the report, and some suggested that the data should be suppressed.[13] Even so, a follow-up of the reported sample group four years later demonstrated no significant differences in relapses of controlled drinkers versus total abstainers.[14] That should have ended the matter; however, the findings were defamed and suppressed. One popularly written book directed toward laypeople went so far as to say:

"Scientifically, the first Rand Report was a disaster," said Dr. Enoch Gordis, the NIAAA's director, when questioned about it in 1987. "On the other hand, the alcoholism field reacted as if heresy had been spoken in church, rather than treating the report as what it really was—a mistake in science."[15]

The Rand Report most assuredly was *not* a "mistake in science." The results have been well-confirmed over time. A growing list of scientific clinical reports indicate that a significant number of former alcoholics can—and do—drink socially and function well for many years. Many have even reported that those alcoholics who drink in moderation[16] are better adjusted than "alcoholic" total abstainers. (I am not hereby recommending even moderate drinking to nondrinkers. Nevertheless, I must be honest and fair with the facts.) Yet the public—and, in particular, the Christian community—remains utterly unaware of this contradiction to disease-concept dogma.

The recovery industry believes that willpower has little if anything to do with the outcome of the alcoholic:

Our sponsors declared that we were the victims of a mental obsession so subtly powerful that no amount of human willpower could break it. There was, they said, no such thing as the personal conquest of this compulsion by the unaided will.[17]

Nevertheless, the vast majority of researchers have concluded that willpower *does* affect the outcome of a drinker's efforts to control his drinking behavior. Studies have shown that it is precisely the characterologic make-up of the individual—his perseverance, his willpower—as opposed to the kind of treatment, that determines whether he will recover.

In deciding whether or not disease-based treatment programs are effective, one must account for the fact that approximately one-third of all alcohol abusers improve over time without any treatment.[18] So a treatment approach must do better than this in order to be considered efficacious.

If successful remission from the "disease" of alcoholism is defined by abstinence, then treatment programs are certainly not cost-effective, because the vast majority of those treated for alcoholism *do* drink again after treatment.[19] Each year, some heavy drinkers do moderate their intake or choose to abstain for a time. However, no evidence indicates that this phenomenon is in any way related to their participation or nonparticipation in a traditional treatment program.

(I am not suggesting that we need to overcome alcoholism or drug addiction by the "unaided" will. There is considerable help for an addict, not the least of which is the grace of God expressed in many practical ways. Nonetheless, objectivity requires me to acknowledge that even without "outside" help, many addicts *do* recover.)

When one claims that recovery industry dogma is science, one is left with labels and tautologies: "He drinks too much because he is an alcoholic." This gets us nowhere if we want to understand *why* he drinks too much and *how* we can help him drink less. The disease dogma maintains that the alcoholic has no power of choice over taking or not taking the first drink. But in order to enter a disease-based treatment program, the alcoholic must voluntarily stop drinking! If the alcoholic is unable to abstain from drinking, how can a program demand that he do so as a condition of admission? And if he is able to abstain, why does he need treatment?

Research has regularly shown that alcoholics can even outgrow alcoholism on their own and that "self-cure" is common. In the words of Harold Mulford, speaking as director of alcohol studies at the University of Iowa:

> Contrary to the traditional clinical view of the alcoholism disease process, progress in the alcoholic process is neither inevitable nor irreversible. Eventually, the balance of natural forces shifts to decelerate progress in the alcoholic process and to accelerate the rehabilitation process.[20]

Understand that I am *not* saying that former heavy drinkers should *not* become total abstainers. Many who come to Christ from a lifestyle of alcohol abuse want nothing to do with drinking activities and the attendant worldliness and sensuality which often accompany it. They naturally desire to make a complete break with their former lives and thus will often choose a lifestyle of total abstinence. Likewise, some Christians who have slipped into lifestyles including heavy drinking will, in repentance, turn one hundred and eighty degrees. They frequently want to eliminate any activity they believe would hamper their Christian witness and service to the Lord, and so they choose to be total abstainers. Such decisions should be respected. Certainly no one should depreciate them by calling them "legalistic." The Apostle Paul espoused moderation in all things and freedom of choice for each of us in all things that are lawful (1 Corinthians 6:12; 10:23). Therefore, the Biblical pattern is simply to let people choose their own way in the lawful things without making their choice binding on their Christian brothers and sisters.

"BORN THAT WAY"

Disease-concept adherents use several theories to support the belief that alcoholics and drug addicts are born that way.

GENETIC HYPOTHESIS

Much has been written about the role of genetics in the development of "alcoholism." In fact, disease dogma demands a genetic etiology, or origin. In reviewing the research studies on the inheritance of alcoholism, researcher David Lester finds that the studies "suggest that genetic involvement in the etiology of alcoholism . . . is weak at best."[21]

Research on the children of alcoholic parents does demonstrate that they are statistically at much greater risk than average of becoming alcoholics themselves. However, the researchers were forced to admit that they could not distinguish between environment and heredity to explain this increased risk. The studies of identical twins of alcoholic parents who were not raised by either parent (thus eliminating the role of environment) would seem to suggest more strongly a genetic role.

In a widely quoted study, 18 percent of sons who had an alcoholic parent became alcoholics, compared to 5 percent of the sons with no alcoholic parents.[22] But of course, what the researchers failed to point out was that 82 percent of the sons who had an alcoholic parent did not become alcoholics. Thus some sort of genetic factor is possibly present, but its exact role is uncertain and miniscule.

In summary, it seems that:

● genetics may be a factor in predisposition to alcoholism, but its magnitude is unknown.

● the studies have been hampered by differing definitions of alcoholism by the various researchers.

● genetics may be used to predict national rates of alcoholism, but is useless on an individual basis since 82 percent of the time the prediction is not fulfilled.

- whatever the role of heredity, if any, life history and environment appear to be far more important in determining whether or not an individual will ever become a heavy drinker.
- genetic factors do not account for the widely ranging differences between problem and nonproblem drinkers.
- *no* evidence shows that certain individuals become alcoholics as a result of the first drink.

Perhaps the children of heavy drinkers *should* be warned that they may be at risk, to some as yet unspecified degree, of becoming alcohol abusers. But we have no grounds for the optimism expressed by Dr. Boris Tabakoff:

> We are very close to unraveling the biological enigmas of the disease. Even if we do not find a cure for alcoholism, we will probably be able to prevent and arrest it in the future.[23]

How could we be close to unraveling the enigmas of a disease for which there is no evidence of existence?

Nothing grabs the headlines in the newspapers more than a report that someone has found the gene that "causes" alcoholism or drug addiction. At the time of this writing, a scientific study that supposedly proved the existence of such a gene has been debunked by several other scientists.[24]

No one can demonstrate that a gene causes alcoholism, just as no one can demonstrate that a gene causes adultery, lying, thievery, blasphemy, or any other such behavior. These are sinful activities in which we choose to participate rather than diseases we inherit.

I am willing to concede that somebody may someday demonstrate a genetic basis for the fact that certain people seem to enjoy the taste of alcohol more than others. But of what benefit would that discovery be? Some of us appreciate music while others are tone deaf. Some of us enjoy ocean sailing while others become seasick. A genetic basis may account for some of this, but how does such knowledge help us? Many who now enjoy drinking alcoholic beverages had to *learn* to enjoy it—sometimes to their eventual detriment. Some who did not seem to "inherit" a sense of music appreciation have subsequently learned to love music. Such are choices we make and habits we cultivate; genetics has little if anything to do with it.

METABOLIC HYPOTHESIS

Some writers have postulated that alcoholics have a genetically determined biochemical abnormality that causes them to respond to alcohol differently from non-alcoholics. This abnormality supposedly "causes" alcoholism. Admittedly, some studies in the 1970s seemed to indicate that alcoholics had higher blood levels of acetaldehyde (an intermediate metabolic breakdown product of ethanol) than did nonalcoholics.[25] In turn, it was postulated that these higher blood levels somehow produced physical dependence on alcohol. Milam and Ketcham disseminated this theory in the popular book *Under the Influence*. These authors argued that this inherited difficulty in the metabolism of alcohol is genetically determined and is a primary cause of alcoholism. However, no experimental evidence has ever substantiated this, and to my knowledge, no researchers are pursuing this avenue.

Additionally, it has been suggested that alcoholics have higher brain levels of morphine-like substances.[26] According to this theory, acetaldehyde reacts with neurotransmitters in the brain to create products called tetrahydroisoquinolones (TIQs). These substances supposedly influence the way alcoholics experience the effects of drinking alcohol. TIQs are thought to create the intense craving for alcohol that alcoholics seem to demonstrate. Interestingly, this theory contradicts the widely held insensitivity model of addiction—alcoholics increase their alcohol intake because they respond less to its effects. Although most investigators have abandoned this line of research, the TIQ theory is often taught to those undergoing treatment at alcoholism recovery facilities across the United States.

More work on the metabolic "causes" of alcoholism will no doubt be forthcoming, but the evidence thus far indicates that this approach to treatment is just another "dead end." No theory of a metabolic "cause" of alcoholism can possibly suffice because:

● even if it were discovered that the effects of alcohol

were somehow more pleasurable for the alcoholic, this would not account for the drinking *patterns* of heavy drinkers.

● it cannot explain why, after a long period of abstinence, long after these metabolic products have disappeared, alcoholics often resume patterns of alcohol abuse.

● an alcoholic may manifest differences in the way he metabolizes alcohol as the *result* of years of heavy alcohol intake. Metabolic changes may be a consequence of chronic abuse, rather than the *cause* of that abuse.

TOLERANCE AND WITHDRAWAL HYPOTHESIS

Some have postulated that after years of chronic heavy drinking, an alcoholic develops tolerance to alcohol (ever greater amounts of alcohol are required to obtain a given effect). When he ceases drinking, he develops physical symptoms of withdrawal, and in order to alleviate these symptoms, he drinks more alcohol. Thus begins a vicious cycle. Much research has been done on this, but the theory breaks down because:

● it takes many years of chronic heavy use to develop withdrawal symptoms. Why then does one abuse alcohol before these symptoms develop?

● more than one-third of alcoholics never develop physical withdrawal symptoms.

● most alcoholics do not drink while undergoing withdrawal symptoms.

- for many alcoholics, drinking is not followed by relaxation, but rather by depression and anxiety.
- experiments do not demonstrate a necessary correlation of blood alcohol levels and withdrawal symptoms.

PSYCHOLOGICAL HYPOTHESIS

Treatment dogma maintains that addicts have a physical, medical, biochemical etiology for their "disease" of addiction and that psychological disorders, if present, are the result of this "disease." At the same time, many studies have been conducted to search for psychological precursors to chemical dependency. For example, some researchers have found abnormalities in the brain waves of children of alcoholics, children who have never drunk alcohol themselves.[27] However, other factors—psychological or physical abuse—could explain these differences. Furthermore, various researchers have found different abnormalities in the brain waves; yet no consistent abnormal pattern has come to light. Moreover, these children will have to be followed until well past middle age to see if they develop chemical addiction.

Any inherited personality theory holding that chemical addicts are psychologically predisposed to addiction must overcome the insurmountable difficulties involved in ascribing complex personality syndromes (such as a tendency to criminality) to specific genes. While science rejects the biological cause of addiction, almost everyone rejects a pre-addictive abnormal personality as a cause of the addiction. Despite all the studies, theories, and hypotheses, no one has demonstrated the existence of an "alcoholic personality." In his study of the personalities of addicted people, Gerald May states:

> It is true, then, that a particular kind of personality distortion occurs with addiction, not as its cause but as its effect. It is an addict*ed* personality instead of an addict*ive* personality.[28]

One can well imagine that a person whose entire life now revolves around taking the next drink or snorting the next line of cocaine has undergone a change in personality.

CROSS-ADDICTION

One of the most intransigent points of the disease dogma is the concept of cross-addiction. According to this belief, an alcoholic, because of his biochemical make-up, can easily become addicted to any other potentially mood-altering drug in addition to his addiction to alcohol. So deeply ingrained is this concept that people are urged to inform their physicians that they are "alcoholics" and that they must be given no alcohol and no potentially addictive drugs. A woman named Nan Robertson was hospitalized for a very serious illness. Her account of this experience demonstrates the implications of the cross-addiction belief:

Before I slipped into a coma at dawn the next day, I had been awake and aware enough to tell the emergency room doctors that I was a recovered alcoholic, in AA for years. That warned them not to give me addictive drugs or medicine with alcohol as a base. I had been told at Smithers to do that with every new physician. The information went into my hospital record.[29]

The presupposition here is that the alcoholic is biochemically different from nonalcoholics and can become addicted to many different kinds of drugs of radically differing molecular structures. No articles from scientific journals can be cited here because there is absolutely *no* evidence for this. People who abuse alcohol may also abuse other mood-altering chemicals for their effects. The most that can be said for this phenomenon is a tautology: People who like to "get high" like to "get high."

To illustrate the absurdity of this whole line of reasoning, Stanton Peele retells the story of baseball player Dwight Gooden.[30] The athlete was forced to endure inpatient drug "treatment" when he tested positive for cocaine in 1987. He had no trouble refraining from its use while pitching because, although he obviously enjoyed the effects of cocaine, he was not addicted to it. He was told that the first use of a drug means one is "starting" to be addicted to it, so he was incarcerated in a treatment facility for "starting to be addicted" to cocaine. When he related his take-it-or-leave-it attitude toward cocaine use, he was accused of lying. Gooden was later excoriated for drinking beer and claiming, ". . . beer's not a problem for me." Although the party line of the recovery industry was that he was an addict/alcoholic and that he must forever abstain from the use of all mood-altering chemicals, Gooden was having no part of the myth. (As a clinician and physician, I would have to say that *all* nonmedicinal use of drugs such as cocaine is abuse and is therefore wrong. Gooden was in sin, not sickness, when he used cocaine.)

Even some in the recovery industry have problems accommodating the cross-addiction idea. Robertson quotes one AA member as saying:

> This fellowship was formed to help suffering alcoholics, and alcoholics only. That's why it has been so successful—we don't monkey around with other problems. I don't feel that the problems of alkies and addicts are interchangeable.[31]

Some communities have even formed "Over Thirty" groups—the clear implication being that no drug addicts are welcome. One can often find "closed" AA meetings for alcoholics only. Therefore, some drug counselors tell drug addicts to say they are both alcoholics and drug addicts. This looseness with the truth accommodates the cross-addiction myth. It does not, however, help the alcoholic or drug addict.

DENIAL

Denial is the "symptom" of chemical addiction that makes it impossible for the chemically dependent to "recognize" their problems or admit to being addicted. The addict, according to this view, is in a state of delusion that keeps him or her from seeing reality. One problem with the recovery industry definition of denial is that it can be used to prove that almost anyone is an addict. Nonaddicts would naturally deny being addicted. Would they then be denying reality or affirming the truth? Conversely, what about all those addicts who readily admit their addiction. Are they not addicted?

Also, denial of what one knows to be true is not necessarily due to delusion. That is, one may deny the truth for a variety of reasons. The person may wish to deceive others. A bank robber may deny to the police that he has robbed the bank. Does that mean, therefore, that he is convinced of his innocence? I suspect that many, if not most, addicts who deny their addiction *have* admitted it to themselves. Their denial does not stem from failure to accept their addiction; instead it results from their desire to prevent others from considering them addicts.

What are we to say about the man falsely accused of robbing the bank? If denial is an indication of guilt, then all who deny guilt are guilty. But if this were so, confession of addiction would indicate innocence. That is, the one who admits to addiction must not be addicted. Sound silly? It should, because it is. If both the guilty and the innocent are likely to deny guilt, denial only proves that denial proves nothing.

One may even think of reasons why the nonaddicted may choose to confess to addictions they do not have. For example, if a judge requires a person convicted of driving while intoxicated to undergo "successful" treatment in order to get his license reinstated, he may admit to being an alcoholic. If he refuses to do so, he may never have his license returned. Likewise, a man convicted of a crime he did not commit (perhaps as the result of being framed) may admit guilt if he believes that by so doing he may get a lighter sentence. When the recovery industry believes those who confess addiction, it inadvertently admits that denial does not necessarily indicate addiction.

Denial is actually a foundational aspect of the human condition. It goes all the way back to the Garden of Eden when Adam said, ". . . it was the woman you gave to me . . ." (Genesis 3:12). Adam denied his responsibility for his sinful act and shifted blame to the woman (and, ultimately, to God). We all have a bent toward denying culpability for our actions, and we soon become very proficient at doing so. Why does it surprise anyone that an addict will deny his addiction? All of us use denial, and it is certainly not the symptom of a disease.

CONCLUSION

The disease model proponents want us to believe that all that we know about addiction treatment comes from years of scientific research. But it is clear to anyone who studies the evidence that the assumptions of the disease model of addiction are false and in fact prevent us from effectively dealing with the problem. The disease model has a number of adverse consequences.

● People are taught concepts that fly in the face of scientific research. When people rigidly hold beliefs despite all evidence to the contrary, we need to call these beliefs what they are—delusions.

● Resources are squandered on a very small group of heavy drinkers (labeled "alcoholics"), giving the majority of heavy drinkers an excuse for denying their drinking problems.

● The medical model of a physical disease ignores the moral and spiritual aspects of drinking behavior, thus allowing the alcohol abuser to escape responsibility for his conduct.

● It requires a lifelong program with a permanent addict identity. Persons involved in such programs are possibly more likely to relapse. Certainly they are more likely to relapse if their rigid, stereotyped routine is disrupted.

● Lifelong treatment and lifelong abstinence take a toll on people. They develop other addictions: to coffee, to tobacco, even to the Twelve Step group itself.

- It attacks the core of one's capacity for self-control. People who decide that their behavior is a symptom of an irreversible disease process feel that it is impossible to resist the addiction.
- The natural result of the addict identity is that the person associates with others having the same identity. People preoccupied with their disease, who blame their failures on it, are poor role models.
- It introduces an exceedingly frustrating paradox. People are told they have a disease that prevents them from exercising self-control in their drinking habits, but that they must exercise self-control by totally abstaining from alcohol in order to keep from succumbing to the disease.

From a Scriptural point of view, calling the sin of alcoholism or drug addiction a sickness can never be acceptable. Even from a scientific point of view, however, there is no good reason for embracing the disease concept. Conversely, from a scientific perspective there is every reason to reject it altogether.

Nevertheless, when writers in this field continue to promote the disease concept, the public's misinformed view is a little more understandable. For example, Sandra Shaw and Durk Pearson, co-authors of a book about alcohol addiction entitled *Life Extension*, maintain:

Alcohol addiction is not due to weak will or moral depravity; it is a genetic metabolic defect ... [just like the] genetic metabolic defect resulting in gout.[32]

Again, this statement merely lets the substance abuser off the moral hook. It makes him feel like a victim. After all, we don't hold a person morally accountable for a defective metabolism. An article appearing in the *Newsletter of the Alcoholism Council of Greater New York* expresses this tragically misguided view. It said:

> . . . the derelict . . . , intent only on . . . getting sufficient booze . . . [is] the victim of metabolism, a metabolism the derelict is born with, a metabolic disorder that causes excessive drinking.[33]

Notice that it is not excessive drinking that causes his problem, but his problem causes excessive drinking. How can we expect derelicts to assume responsibility when the message we send them is that they cannot be held accountable?

Scripture tells us what alcohol and drug addiction is: sin. Thus, by implication, it tells us what it is not: sickness. Science tells us what alcohol and drug addiction is not: sickness. Everyone agrees that addiction is "bad." It is bad in either one of two ways. It is bad as small pox is bad. This is essentially the view of the recovery industry. Or it is bad as lying is bad. This is essentially the view of Biblical Christianity.

Science tells us it is *not* bad like small pox (a disease).

Scripture tells us it *is* bad like lying (sin).

To paraphrase a line in a popular movie: "Who you

gonna believe?" The truth of God's Word, or the pseudo-scientific notions of the recovery industry?

The inculcation of the addict identity among those who are remorseful, defeated, and ashamed of their conduct in any other context would be called brainwashing. Note this from Enoch Gordis:

> In the case of alcoholism, our whole treatment system, with its innumerable therapies, armies of therapists, large and expensive programs, endless conferences . . . and public relations activities is founded on hunch, not evidence, and not on science. . . . Yet the history of medicine demonstrates repeatedly that unevaluated treatment, no matter how compassionately administered, is frequently useless and wasteful and sometimes dangerous or harmful. The lesson we have learned is that *what is plausible may be false, and what is done sincerely may be useless or worse.*[34]

In conclusion, the failure of research to find one single, unitary causal explanation for "alcoholism" has a very positive outcome: we can now abandon the futile search for a nonexistent disease and begin to deal realistically with alcohol and drug abuse. Alcoholics and drug addicts need no longer see themselves as victims of some accident of nature. They are normal people caught up in destructive behavior patterns—they have bad habits, not bad genes. They do not need treatment for a sickness;

they need to turn from sin. If pastors called upon polio victims to repent for polio, we would rightfully consider this a form of spiritual malpractice. But is it not a form of medical malpractice when the recovery industry excuses the sin of chemical abuse as sickness?

Four

Your Dollars at Work:

The Failure of the Recovery Industry

I f the goal of the recovery industry is to help addicts stop abusing alcohol or drugs, then its success or failure ought to be measured by how well it does so. However, even if we were to concede that the recovery industry "works," that would not necessarily make it "right." Heroin will most assuredly get rid of a headache, but it has other serious and undesirable side effects, and its use for that purpose is illegal. As Christians, we must consider the means as well as the ends. But not only are the means and message of the recovery industry wrong; they do not work. Thus when the church adopts recovery industry practices, it is compromised by that industry's methods and follows it into failure.

It would be impossible to discuss the "success" rate of the recovery industry intelligently without referring to

Alcoholics Anonymous. After all, the industry is to a great extent a reflection of the views and practices of that organization. William E. Mayer, M.D., Director of the Alcohol, Drug Abuse, and Mental Health Administration says, "AA, by and large works better than anything we have been able to devise with all our science and all our money and all our efforts."[1] Because Mayer's views are shared by so many, the Christian recovery ministry has been greatly influenced by AA practices.

No one is more convinced of AA's success than AA itself. As a matter of fact, AA says: "Rarely have we seen a person fail who has thoroughly followed our path."[2]

Is that optimism justified? Hardly.

THE UNHELPABLE

In order to explain those cases in which it fails, AA has theorized a special category of an alcoholic *beyond* help. In other words, if the individual were helpable, AA could help. By definition, however, no one can help the unhelpable. As Bill W., co-founder of AA, contends:

Those who do not recover [following the AA path] are people who cannot or will not completely give themselves to this simple program, usually men and women who are constitutionally incapable of being honest with themselves. There are such unfortunates.

They are not at fault; they seem to be born that way. They are naturally incapable of grasping and developing a manner of living which demands rigorous honesty.[3]

Obviously, if someone is "constitutionally incapable," the individual cannot take advantage of the help offered by AA. Thus, it would be logically unfair to include these in a discussion of AA's success/failure rate—the "normal" alcoholic cannot be faulted for being an alcoholic, only for not getting help. This "abnormal" alcoholic cannot even get help. A really hopeless case if there ever was one.

To understate the case, many people share the views of Stanley Gitlow, a clinical professor of medicine at Mt. Sinai School of Medicine and chairperson of the Committee on Alcoholism of the Medical Society of New York. He expresses the conventional wisdom on the subject, and anyone who disagrees seems somehow out of step. According to Dr. Gitlow:

AA is the most effective means of teaching an alcoholic how to stop drinking that I know of.[4]

If AA were as successful as it claims to be, it should also welcome outside observers from the scientific community to evaluate its program objectively. But as Herbert Fingarette says:

Despite the ubiquitous good opinion of AA, there are no satisfactory data to justify the widespread confidence in it, in part because AA has long been reluctant to gather or publish statistics.[5]

What is it, might we ask, that AA does not want the public to know? Is there something to hide? Would such a study of the records prove embarrassing or even worse for AA? Despite AA's reluctance, there are ways for the scientific community to verify the claims of AA and of the recovery industry as a whole.

AA's glowing reputation for success has not kept it from having detractors, especially among medical science researchers. Stanton Peele points out that:

The actual scientific evidence, however, strongly *contradicts* the contentions of the alcoholism movement. For example, the standard wisdom is that AA is unmatched in effectiveness for dealing with alcoholism and that alcoholism would be licked if only everyone joined AA.[6]

Some of the scientific evidence against AA's contentions came from the Downstate Medical Center Department of Psychiatry in New York:

The general applicability of AA as a treatment method is much more limited than has been supposed in the past. Available data do not support AA's claims of much higher success rates than clinic treatment. Indeed, when population differences are taken into account, the reverse seems to be true.[7]

According to Peele:

> Not one study has ever found AA or its derivatives to be superior to any other approach, or even to be better than not receiving any help at all. . . .[8]

If AA is not successful in helping solve the nation's problem of alcohol abuse, it has certainly been successful in convincing everyone it is well on its way to doing so. Is this true? If not, why hasn't the public caught on by now?

Peele may have part of the answer when he says:

> The universal praise for AA focuses on its successes and disregards its failures, while we hear little about the successful recovery of those who don't attend AA. People who overcome drinking problems on their own, despite their numbers, are not an organized and visible group on the American alcoholism landscape.[9]

According to Fingarette, "The public is often impressed by the argument that drinkers who do persist in AA remain abstinent."[10] However, that argument has serious flaws. Fingarette comments, "Drinkers remain in AA only if they are able to remain reasonably abstinent and also accept the AA way of life. The vast majority of heavy drinkers never try AA, and most who do join drop out."[11]

This is not to suggest that because alcoholics drop out of AA the AA program is necessarily a bad program. I believe it is bad, but not for that reason. I bring it up only because it is a necessary part of the equation. The large number who come to AA for help and drop out or relapse—as well as the even larger number who for whatever reason never come—prove that AA is not the panacea it is often made out to be.

In an honest and accurate assessment of AA and the recovery industry we must include those who will not come for help as well as those who do come and are not helped. Regarding those who do not submit to AA for treatment—all other things being equal, severity and duration of addiction and so on—we must ask the question: Do they do better, worse, or about the same as those who *do* submit to treatment? Among those who do come for help we must consider how many succeed or fail to be helped over the long haul.

Fingarette points out that the AA program of recovery is not acceptable to the majority of people who have problems resulting from alcohol abuse. As a result of this:

> Selectivity in the kind of drinkers who enter a treatment regimen biases the outcomes and precludes any generalization about the regimen's success with heavy drinkers or problem drinkers at large. Drinkers who

become active participants in AA are those who are willing to affirm themselves as alcoholics under the AA definition; drinkers who do not fit or will not acknowledge fitting the pattern drop out.[12]

What is true of AA treatment is evidently true of other disease-oriented recovery programs. There is simply no evidence to substantiate the claims for success. While the recovery industry is going to great lengths to convince us how helpful it is, the facts actually prove the contrary. According to Peele:

> . . . the research on treatment paints a very different picture. It has been remarkably hard to find systematic proof that treatment for alcoholism and other addictions accomplishes *anything at all.*[13]

Evidence is now in from both proponents as well as recovery industry opponents, that treatment is not working. Note this conclusion by treatment proponent Dr. George Vaillant, who did an eight-year comparison of his treatment results with the remission rates of untreated alcoholics:

> . . . there is compelling evidence that the results of our treatment were no better than the natural history of the disease.[14]

By "natural history of the disease," Vaillant means the progression of alcoholism—or drug addiction—from the onset of problems to the ending of those problems without intervention or treatment as such. In other words, without the help of the recovery industry, the nontreated alcoholic did as well as those who received help. Concerning his earlier work, Vaillant concluded:

> The best that can be said for our exciting treatment . . . is that we were certainly not interfering with the normal recovery process.[15]

Again, the "normal recovery process" refers to recovery without "help" from the recovery industry. That is to say, without treatment of any kind.

Of course, some people in recovery programs do succeed in getting sober and staying sober. But when one considers that treatment is very expensive, that treated addicts do no better than untreated ones, and that the Christian in disease-oriented "treatment" often must deny what Scripture says about his condition, one must conclude that "treatment" extracts too great a price for so little or no return. Besides, as Fingarette notes:

> Differences of opinion exist among research authorities, but the basic finding of diverse studies and reviews of the literature is that if traditional alcoholism recovery programs help at all, it is not because of specific medical or nonmedical regimen. Whatever

value these recovery programs have is modest at best, and it seems to reside not in the programs' particular techniques but in whatever practical advice and personal support they may give.[16]

One does not need the recovery industry to find "practical advice and personal support." Certainly the church ought to be able to provide far more.

Trying hard to give the recovery industry every benefit of a doubt, Fingarette says:

> In the aggregate, then, the strongest scientifically based claims that can be made by disease-oriented recovery programs is that the staff try to be supportive and helpful and that doing something may perhaps be a bit more effective—or at least no worse—than doing nothing for chronic heavy drinkers seeking assistance in controlling their drinking behavior.[17]

On balance then, it would seem that our individual and collective investment in the recovery industry yields a very unsatisfactory return. We do not get a statistically better chance of achieving and maintaining sobriety from the recovery industry. What we do get is the propagation and perpetuation of the disease myth and all that accompanies the embracing of this myth. Surely, as Christians, we can and ought to be doing better, at least for our own, than doing "no worse."

The pseudoscientific disease concept is now recognized by science for what it really is: a lie. It is time for the general public and especially the Christian community to be brought in out of the dark.

Of course, the bottom line for the believer should always be, "What does Scripture say?" But even if we set aside the rightness or truth of the disease-based recovery industry, we still must give it a failing grade. If you bought a vacuum cleaner that did not actually pick up dirt, would you say it worked? What would you say to the vacuum cleaner salesperson who said, "It may not help, but neither does it hurt"? I doubt you would knowingly spend one thin dime on such a product. In effect, this is the kind of problem we face with the recovery industry. No matter how we evaluate it, the treatment simply does not work "as advertised." The cost and the stakes, of course, are much higher when dealing with people's lives. We have much more to lose than a financial investment.

Five

The Legacy of a Useful Lie:

Why the Disease Concept Prevails

I f the disease concept is debunked by science, one may ask, why does the recovery industry continue to embrace it? Further, why do we not hear more from the scientific community in general, and medical science researchers in particular, about the unscientific nature of the disease concept of alcohol and drug addiction?

These important questions yield some disturbing answers. One reason for referring to alcoholism or drug addiction as a disease is that it is a useful lie. Convinced of the utilitarian value of the disease concept, one proponent said:

> Calling alcoholism a disease, rather than a behavior disorder, is a useful device both to persuade the alco-

holic to admit his alcoholism [or drug addiction] and to provide a ticket for admission into the health care system.[1]

I do not doubt that calling a sin "sickness" makes it much easier for some to *admit* addiction. This, however, is like calling the act of stealing a car "borrowing" because it will be easier to get a confession. In some ways it is like plea bargaining—a man who committed a felony admits to a misdemeanor. However, even in plea bargaining, a criminal admits to a crime, albeit a lesser one. Many people are troubled by this practice because it redefines the concept of justice in the criminal justice system. Some have gone so far as to suggest the phrase "criminal justice" has become an oxymoron because of the prevalence of plea bargaining. Be that as it may, the disease concept has gone even farther—it altogether lets the sinner off the moral and spiritual hook. What guilt is there, after all, in being sick?

So calling alcoholism and drug addiction diseases provides "a ticket into the health care system." However, is this honest? Is this where we want them? Is this going to do them any good?

Note that the same man who said calling alcoholism a disease is a "useful device" also said:

> I willingly concede . . . in scientific terms *behavior disorder* will often be a happier semantic choice than *disease*.[2]

This is like saying don't confuse laypeople with the facts or the truth about chemical dependency. What they don't know won't hurt them. Unfortunately, it does hurt the addict.

This is a very sorry state of affairs. Christians especially should be interested in the truth. After all, it is the truth, not a useful lie, that sets people free.

The alcoholism and drug addiction recovery industry has a great deal to lose if the word gets out that this "disease" notion is the moral equivalent of the emperor's new clothes. If there is no disease, then there is nothing to treat. Workers in the field, not to mention the multibillion dollar businesses built upon this false premise, are needed only if the "alcoholic" and drug addict require medical care. Thus:

> To ensure continued public support and funding, the alcoholism [and drug addiction] recovery programs have formed national, state, and local umbrella organizations that publicize their efforts and lobby elected officials and influential citizens. From the National Council on Alcoholism on down, these politically oriented organizations form a truly powerful and ubiquitous pressure group. And because the majority of the treatment programs are based on the disease concept of alcoholism, their lobbying, public relations, and advertising efforts inevitably propagate the disease theme.[3]

This is not to suggest that these organizations and the people who represent them do not subscribe to the disease concept. Certainly many, if not most, are quite sincere. Rather, I am saying only that big bucks play a big role in how much the recovery industry is willing to do in order to protect and preserve intact the disease concept. The pressure felt by those who "know better" and might wish to say something about it is considerable. In fact, pressure acts as a very effective censor. After all, medical science researchers need funding to do their research. They are between the proverbial rock and a hard place. Remember that they receive funding from the very industry their research calls into question.

But the dilemma goes beyond funding:

> The classic disease concept remains the cornerstone of traditional treatment and public opinion, the central premise of media coverage and social debate, such that anyone who publicly doubts or challenges the disease concept is likely to be ignored, dismissed or ostracized. In this version of the emperor's new clothes, truthfulness can threaten, block, or ruin the truthteller's career.[4]

Perhaps the most important of all reasons the disease concept dominates the recovery industry is a very subjective and personal one. That is, in most cases recovery industry workers are graduates of recovery industry programs dominated by the disease concept. To challenge the disease concept is, for many, to challenge their own recovery from addiction. Fingarette explains:

> One key factor is the widespread presence in the treatment and lobbying communities of para-professional staff members who define themselves as "recovering alcoholics." Indeed, the largest single category of direct service staff in programs specifically concerned with alcohol [or drugs] consists of counselors without professional degrees, many of whom were once heavy drinkers [or drug addicts] and now claim special qualification to help others by reason of their own experience. Since their own treatment was effected at a time when the classic disease concept of alcoholism was dominant, they tend to have faith in the old dogma and tend to perceive any challenge to the disease concept as a challenge to the validity of their own emotional ordeal and conversion to sobriety.[5]

The future dominance of the disease concept in the recovery industry is all but assured, as long as industry workers—and the general public—are convinced that the "treatment" works reasonably well. It is said that if recovery industry's methodology is based upon the premise that alcoholism and drug addiction are diseases, and if the recovery industry is successful—the disease concept must be given a lion's share of the credit for that success.

However, the so-called useful lie turns out to be useful only in the sense that most lies are useful: it misleads. More importantly, it misleads by drawing us away from the truth—the only thing that can set us free. It also leads us into the lie that we have a sickness instead of a sin. We would do well to pray with the psalmist, "Oh Lord . . . lead me in your truth" (Psalm 25:5).

Part 2

Six

Christianized Compromise:

Addicted to Addiction

To say that many Christians are enamored with the recovery industry would be putting it mildly. Alternative treatment groups are springing up in churches all across the nation, and Christian publishers have practically created a whole new category of books spinning off bestsellers in droves. As it turns out, many of these "alternatives" are merely extensions of the secular recovery industry. While the church sends its members to this industry for treatment, the recovery industry in turn tells the church what to believe and do about alcohol and drug addiction. As one advocate of these "Christianized" alternatives admits:

> These groups are NOT intended to replace Alcoholics Anonymous, Al-Anon, etc., but are a supplementary program. . . .[1]

Rather than allow God's Word and wisdom to direct and shape the church's policies about addictive and destructive behaviors, many are content merely to rely upon the recovery industry. Some Christians go even further and suggest that the recovery industry does not even need the church for supplementary purposes. They believe that the industry is adequate in and of itself to handle their addiction problems. For example, Alexander DeJong, who is both a Christian and a treatment "expert," says that "AA provides a simple and sound program that any alcoholic can follow."[2]

I'm certain DeJong would think the same way about Narcotics Anonymous for Christian drug addicts, Al-Anon, Al-Ateen, and even—yes—Al-Atot for the loved ones of the chemically dependent.

DeJong explains why he believes Christians with alcohol and drug addiction problems, or Christians who have loved ones who are addicted, need not look for a Christ-centered alternative:

> . . . I'm often asked whether born-again believers ought to form their own groups. In answering both co-alcoholics who often attend Al-Anon meetings and alcoholics who attend closed meetings, I call attention to these facts: attendance at meetings is fluid. One can move freely from one group to another. If one is not entirely comfortable with a certain group, he should try attending somewhere else. We urge each other to shop around for a meeting which fits.

. . . I do not feel that special Christian groups are needed.[3]

The two things most common to the entire recovery industry are the disease concept of sin (see chapters 1 and 2) and the Twelve Step recovery program of AA. So when Christians come to that industry for treatment, often they unwittingly side with it against Biblical Christianity concerning the true cause and nature of addiction.

For example, DeJong says:

. . . many active alcoholics [or drug addicts] who are Christians remain hopelessly caught in the snare of their illness because they (and the Christian community which surrounds them) feel that their sickness is sin.[4]

Believing what the Bible teaches is considered a *hindrance* rather than a help! I am not saying that most Christian advocates of the recovery industry intend to side against God's Word, but only that adopting the industry's beliefs and practices unavoidably puts them on the wrong side.

Another Christian stated essentially the same view in a slightly different manner: "An alcoholic's recovery is usually connected with his ability to perceive his addiction as a disease."[5]

Typical of the blending of church programs and the

recovery industry approach is a ministry to the chemically dependent called Rapha. It has published *Rapha's Twelve Step Program for Overcoming Chemical Dependency*. The front cover says that the Rapha Twelve Step Program is "a new Christ-centered adaptation of the most successful approach to recovery ever devised."[6]

This, of course, is a reference to AA's Twelve Steps. One wonders why such a "successful approach" needs to be adapted? Rapha attempts to Christianize AA's Twelve Steps in order to make the Christian more comfortable with the AA program of recovery. To illustrate how this is done, compare AA's Step Two with Rapha's.

Step 2

AA—We make a decision to turn our will and lives over to the care of God as we understand Him.

Rapha—We make a decision to turn our lives over to God through Jesus Christ.[7]

The irony of a Twelve Step program customized for Christians is that many who use it believe it is not only effective but Biblical. The author of Rapha's program explains that:

> *Rapha's Twelve Step Program for Overcoming Chemical Dependency* is designed . . . to complement the original Biblically based Twelve Steps of Alcoholics Anonymous.[8]

If the original Twelve Step program needs to be "adapted" for Christians, it seems odd to say it is "Biblically based." What kind of double talk is going on here? Unfortunately, this kind of confusion is characteristic of the literature of "Christianized" recovery programs.

After all is said and done, Christians do not seem to be making the recovery industry approach more compatible with Biblical Christianity. On the contrary, the recovery industry seems to be influencing the Christian approach. The degree to which we turn to the recovery industry in whatever form—whether supposedly Christ-centered or not—is the degree to which we actually turn away from Christ. Where in the Christ-centered alternatives can you find the Christ "in whom" Paul said ". . . are hidden all the treasures of wisdom and knowledge" (Colossians 2:3)?

The sad truth is that many Christians have lost sight of what is hidden in (and only in) Christ.

Seven

The Myth of Christian Origins:

Alcoholics Anonymous

Many within the Christian community believe that the founders of AA were Christians and that AA's Twelve Steps are based on the Bible. The "Higher Power"—"God as you understand him"—referred to in the Twelve Steps is, according to this myth, none other than the Most High and only God of Biblical revelation. However, nothing in AA's history supports these beliefs. In fact, the myth is actually denied by the founders themselves as well as by the official literature of AA and spinoff organizations.

THE TWELVE STEPS—HOW BIBLICAL?

The official literature of AA, as well as the official literature of AA spinoff groups such as Al-Anon, frankly agree that the Twelve Steps are not now *nor have they ever been* Christian. They do not derive exclusively or even primarily from truths or concepts found in either the Old or New Testament. One cannot find anything even remotely similar to the Twelve Steps in the writings of ancient or modern Christian theologians. The secular nature of the Twelve Steps is, in fact, freely admitted by AA groups. Al-Anon, for instance, plainly asserts:

> The Twelve Steps . . . although spiritually oriented, are not based on a specific religious discipline. They embrace not only the philosophies of the Judeo-Christian faiths and the many religions of the East, but nonreligious, ethical and moral thought as well. . . .[1]

As a matter of fact, AA's Twelve Steps are more akin to the Bahai faith than to Biblical Christianity. That is, they are eclectic—a hodge podge of different, and even conflicting, philosophical and religious systems.

However, Biblical Christianity claims to be the only true religion. Such amalgamations as the Twelve Steps have always been spurned by the orthodox Christian community.

Jesus said, "Enter through the narrow gate. For wide is the gate and broad is the road that leads to destruction, and many enter through it. But small is the gate and narrow the road that leads to life, and only a few find it" (Matthew 7:13-14).

Compare this with what co-founder Bill W. said with regard to the AA way: "To us, the Realm of the Spirit is broad, roomy, all inclusive; never exclusive or forbidding. . . ."[2]

THE FOUNDERS—HOW CHRISTIAN?

Just to ask if founders Bill W. and Dr. Bob were Christians seems an insult to many. Of course they were. Look at all the good they did. They started a spiritual movement and a spiritual program. They believed in God, etc. Usually those who claim the founders were Christians do not know what *Christian* means in the Biblical sense, using the word in a way different from what would be accepted by orthodox believers. Nor do these people know much about the lives of Bill W. and Dr. Bob.

Doing good and improving society, to whatever degree the unregenerate are capable of it, may be commendable, but do not make the persons Christian. One could even do much of what the Bible commands and still not be a Christian.

When I use the word *Christian*, I mean one who has personally received Jesus Christ as Lord and Savior into his or her life, one who believes Jesus died for his or her sins and rose bodily from the grave, one who believes Jesus Christ is the one and only way to the Father. A true Christian is both regenerated by the Spirit (born again) and justified (declared righteous) by faith.

I realize that this is much too narrow a definition for many, but it is in keeping with the clear teaching of Scripture. All Christians believe that there is just one true God (monotheism), but not all who believe there is one true God are Christians. To be a Christian in the Biblical sense means one must believe in His one and only eternal Son—Jesus Christ (cf. 1 John 2:22-23).

THE HIGHER POWER vs. THE MOST HIGH

Is the Higher Power of AA the Most High of Biblical Christianity? Not according to Bill W. who seems to bend over backwards to make sure no one would make that connection. The Biblical view of God was too narrow, too restrictive for him. He was understandably worried that if non-Christians believed that the Twelve Steps referred to the Judeo-Christian God, they would not be interested in AA. He intended the concept of "God" to be so generalized and flexible that even atheists and agnostics would not be turned off by it. He said:

> Any number of alcoholics are bedeviled by the dire conviction that if ever they go near AA, they will be pressured to conform to some particular brand of faith or theology. They just don't realize that faith is never an imperative for AA membership; that sobriety can be achieved with an easily acceptable minimum of it, and that our concepts of a Higher Power

and God—as we understand him—afford everyone a nearly unlimited choice of spiritual belief and action. In talking to a prospect, stress the spiritual feature freely. If the man be agnostic or atheist, make it emphatic that he does not have to agree with your conception of God. He can choose any conception he likes, provided it makes sense to him. The main thing is that he is willing to believe in a Power greater than himself and that he live by spiritual principles.[3]

AA and the rest of the recovery industry take this "unlimited choice" very seriously. Anything goes when it comes to the recovery industry "god." In the AA publication *The Clergy Ask About Alcoholics Anonymous* appears the statement:

> We suggest that you find a substitute for this destructive power, alcohol, and turn to a Higher Power, regardless of the name by which you may identify that power. We suggest that you turn your will and your life over to God, *as you understand Him.*[4]

This should not be considered a simple question of what you call God—or by what name you refer to Him. As Al-Anon admits:

> Those who do not subscribe to a particular faith can still find in this program a serene, fulfilling way of life,

if they can believe in any Power greater than themselves.[5]

This *any* power of AA and the recovery industry is really
just that—any power, imagined or real.

Continuing its message to the clergy, AA concedes
that:

> Some members of the clergy may be shocked to learn
> that an agnostic or an atheist may join the Fellowship,
> or to hear an AA [member] say: "I can't accept that
> 'God concept'; I put my faith in the AA group; that's
> my higher power, and it keeps me sober!"[6]

The idea of the AA group as the Higher Power or god
of an AA member should not be shrugged off as hypo-
thetical or even all that exceptional. Recovery industry
literature is replete with testimonials of this kind. For
example, in the AA publication *Came to Believe*, we
read:

> In Step Two, the "Power greater than ourselves"
> meant AA, but not just the members I knew. It meant
> all of us. . . .[7]

Bill W. himself made clear that when AA uses the terms
"God" or "Higher Power," it does not have any particular being in mind at all. It is a kind of "you-fill-in-the-

blank" concept. In effect it is only a *term* that one can do with as he pleases. As Bill W. says:

> . . . the designation "God" [does not] refer to a particular being, force or concept, but only to "God" as each of us understands that *term*. (emphasis mine)[8]

To illustrate how absurd this any-god-will-do idea is, let us assume that I have an addiction to an imaginary substance called Corabine. This addiction is extremely destructive to me, as well as being disruptive for my friends and family. Unless I can become free of this addiction, Corabine will destroy me. It is only a matter of time. I know all this and want to get off the stuff. I quit all the time but can't seem to stay away from using Corabine.

Then I run into an old Corabine buddy with whom I often got high. He told me he was no longer using Corabine, and I was impressed to say the least. His Corabine habit was even worse than mine. So before he could volunteer the information, I asked how he managed to do it. He said that after he hit rock bottom, he turned to god for help. My immediate response was that I did not know he was a religious man. He assured me he was not. He went on to tell me I could live a spiritual life without being religious. When I told him I did not believe in God, he said that was okay too; if I could believe in *any power greater than myself*, it would be enough.

He went on to explain that with the help of other former Corabine abusers and any Higher Power, a god as I understand him, I could get off and stay off, Corabine. I said I would like to give this "god" thing a try. I asked if he thought this god would also help me? He responded that he was certain of it if I were sincere and serious about getting off and staying off Corabine and if I were willing to turn my will and life over to him. I told him I would do anything to be free of this addiction. I asked him what I had to do and how I should turn my life and will over to this god and make him my god.

My friend went on to tell me I could believe anything I wanted to about god, call him what I want or choose any god I want. "ANY GOD WILL DO—SO LONG AS HE IS GREATER THAN YOU."

This analogy represents the exact nature of the problem Christians face with AA and the recovery industry. If we say any god will do so long as he is greater than you, we may open the door for Satan himself.

Why is it so easy for us to call Hinduism, Buddhism, Mormonism, or Shintoism a false religion and not the religion of AA or the recovery industry? AA and the recovery industry's doctrine of God is clearly just as false.

I have never read anything in AA literature or elsewhere to clearly indicate that Bill W. or Dr. Bob were Christians in the Biblical sense. I have read a great deal in AA literature and elsewhere to convince me they were not.

Even if we failed to take into account their amalgamation of religions or their "any-god-will-do" view, it would still be difficult to call them Christians. With the exception of some influence of the controversial Oxford Group Movement, most of the religious influences that helped shape the thinking of the AA founders were anything but Christian. Bill W. and Dr. Bob were religious; that I do not doubt. To call them Christian would, however, be the equivalent of calling a Buddhist or a Mormon Christian.

In *Not-God: A History of Alcoholics Anonymous*, Ernest Kurtz (in many ways a strong supporter of AA and Bill W.) points out that:

> Evidence of the reality of "the spiritual" fascinated Bill W. . . . drawn through friendship with philosopher-mystic Gerald Heard into the ambit of the later-life interests of Aldous Huxley, Wilson experimented with and eventually claimed some power over spiritualistic phenomena. So profound was Bill's immersion in this area that he at times confused the terms "spiritualism" and "spirituality."[9]

As a matter of record, Bill W.'s "interest in spiritualism" was accompanied by "his experimentation with L.S.D."[10] None of this is meant to suggest that AA endorses Wilson's spiritualism or his use of L.S.D. On the contrary, it has gone out of its way to keep information about his involvement in these activities from AA membership.

Those *acknowledged* by AA to be the most important in shaping the many religious aspects of AA were anything but Christian believers in the orthodox sense. This is of course also heavily reflected in the literature of AA. In fact, the most striking evidence of the non-Christian nature of AA is in the testimonials of its members. In *Came to Believe,* which we are told is a record of "the spiritual adventure of AA as experienced by individual members,"[11] not one single testimonial out of the several hundreds could clearly and unquestionably be considered Christian. Not one single reference to the God and Father of Jesus Christ or Jesus Christ, as the one and only Savior, can be found. This is especially interesting when one realizes that every other kind of god is mentioned, and every other kind of testimony is recorded. Out of the millions of AA members, surely AA could have included *one* Christian testimony in a book filled with testimonies! If anything, this book shows an anti-Christian bias.

Members acknowledge Allah, the Life Force, any power greater than a drunk, the AA group as a whole, etc., but never the Lord God of the Scriptures. Either the number of Christians in AA is so small as to be negligible, or AA editors have chosen to exclude Christian testimonies. I will leave it to the reader to decide for himself which explanation is the correct one. In a letter to none other than Carl Jung, Bill W. writes:

You will also be interested to learn that, in addition to the "spiritual experience," many AAs report a great variety of psychic phenomena, the cumulative weight of which is very considerable. Other members have—following their recovery in AA—been much helped by your practitioners. A few have been intrigued by the *I Ching* and your remarkable introduction to that work.[12]

He then adds, "Please be certain that your place in the affection, and in the history, of our Fellowship is like no other."[13]

That Bill W. acknowledged Carl Jung—a profoundly pagan philosopher—as perhaps the single most important outside religious influence upon AA should be very disturbing to Christians who recommend AA to others.

Another troubling connection links the "New Thought" lecturer Emmet Fox and Alcoholics Anonymous. In *AA's Godparents*, author Igor Sikorsky, Jr., says, "The relationship between AA and Emmet Fox serves as an interesting and well-documented vignette in the early history of the fellowship."[14]

Both Bill W. and Dr. Bob were evidently very impressed by Emmet Fox and his views, so much so that Sikorsky says, "before there was any official AA literature, his work served as the basic text for recovering alcoholics."[15]

According to Sikorsky, the practice of "living one

day at a time" is one of the most important rules in metaphysics and came to AA through the teaching of Emmet Fox, who urged his audiences to "train yourself to be a man or woman who lives one day at a time."[16]

Sikorsky explains the significance of this one-day-at-a-time philosophy as follows:

> From Emmet Fox's emphasis on the fact that thoughts are real things, and that one cannot have one kind of mind and another kind of life, came the pattern of changing based upon a new outlook on life. According to Fox, any thought pattern that is persisted in must sooner or later materialize in a person's outer circumstances.[17]

Surely AA founders were familiar with the views of orthodox and evangelical leaders of their day. Why is there no mention of D. L. Moody or Billy Graham? Because in fact, it is men like Fox, Jung, and Huxley, in contrast to men like Moody or Graham, whose views are reflected in the literature of AA. Fox was a liberal modernist, Jung a believer in oriental religions and mysticism, and Huxley an anti-Christian atheist.

Some have pointed to the Oxford Group Movement and AA's ties to it as proof of the Christian origin of AA and its views. There are a number of problems with this thesis. While the founder of the Oxford Group Movement was no doubt a real Christian, many of his views—especially those that impressed Bill W.

and Dr. Bob.—are highly questionable from a Christian perspective. While it may seem a bit harsh, cult researcher Jan Karel Van Baalen, referred to the Oxford Movement (later called Moral Rearmament) as the Buchmanism *cult*. Whether the Oxford Movement is or is not a cult is not the concern of this book. But what influence the Oxford Group had on AA seems to have been forgotten and overshadowed by other not-so-Christian influences.

Even Dr. Samuel Shoemaker, a pastor once associated with both AA and the Oxford Movement, later repudiated Moral Rearmament for some very anti-Christian views.

Through official AA publications and the publications of spinoff groups—reflecting the views of most of the recovery industry—the sin concept is discounted. Even if one could prove that AA founders were Christians and that AA and the Twelve Steps were based upon Biblical principles, that would not change the fact that the recovery industry as a whole is about as non-Christian as it can get.

Eight
The Panacea:

Twelve Steps to Where?

In the recovery industry—Christian and non-Christian alike—the Twelve Steps (or an adaptation of them) hold a central place in programs for treating addicts. Many Christians who may have doubts about the accuracy or effectiveness of the disease model of addiction nevertheless affirm the truth and value of the Twelve Steps. Since they form such an integral part of the recovery industry and since they are held in such high regard even in Christian circles, it is important to understand the Twelve Steps.

In thinking about the Twelve Steps a number of questions come to mind:

● Are the Twelve Steps dependent on the disease model of addiction?

● What is the philosophical/theological worldview that informs the Twelve Steps? Is it fundamentally Christian? Is it neutral toward Christianity but capable of being harmonized with it? Or is it fundamentally anti-Christian?

● Can the Twelve Steps be adapted for use in Christian treatment programs?

To the first question, are the Twelve Steps dependent on the disease model of addiction? the answer would appear to be yes. We have shown above that with the coming of AA a new model of addiction—the disease model—has arisen which has largely supplanted the traditional model, generally called the moral model. We have discussed the difficulties inherent in the disease model from the point of view of both Scripture and science. We have further shown that disease model-based treatment programs have been no more effective—and perhaps are even less effective—in bringing about recovery from addictions than no program at all.

The Twelve Steps are nothing more than an attempt by AA to devise a program that puts into practice the principles of the disease model. Thus, not only are the Twelve Steps dependent on the disease model of addiction, they are the means by which its principles are put into action in the lives of addicts who turn to the recovery industry for help. Therefore, the same failings that hamstring the disease model of addiction equally encumber the Twelve Steps. This will become clear later as we take a closer look at each step.

The second question, what is the philosophical/ theological worldview that informs the Twelve Steps? is largely answered in the previous chapter. There we saw that rather than being informed by orthodox Christianity, the Twelve Steps exhibit a Bahaist or other syncretistic worldview. Some Christians claim that the Twelve Steps do not espouse any particular worldview at all—that they merely describe the nature of recovery in a way similar to how the laws of mechanical engineering describe the nature of bridge building. We must be very careful when we make such statements, however, since this is the same kind of claim that heavily ideological groups like TM have made about their far-from-innocent programs.

Other Christians have said that although the Twelve Steps are not specifically Christian, they nevertheless express principles consistent with Christianity. Even here we must be careful, for although the Twelve Steps claim to be a means of restoring wholeness to broken lives, there is nothing in them about repentance, which is an essential part of the Christian understanding of coming into wholeness.

If the Twelve Steps are dependent on the disease model of addiction with its attendant difficulties, if they are informed by a worldview that has much more in common with Bahaism than Christianity, if they claim to be consistent with Christian principles but ignore essential aspects of Christianity—then it is hard to see why Christians continue to defend them.

The answer to the third question, can the Twelve Steps be adapted for use in Christian treatment programs? is then a resounding no. This becomes increasingly evident as we look more closely at each step.

Step One says:

1. We admitted we were powerless over alcohol—our lives had become unmanageable.

If this means a person is admitting he could never control the amount and frequency of alcohol consumed, it is simply not true. That claim is both unscriptural and unscientific. Scripture allows people to drink moderately, and *only* moderately. If we drink, we must control the drinking. This, of course, assumes the capability of controlling it.

The Apostle Paul, who consumed alcohol in moderate quantities, said, "I will not be brought under the power of anything" (1 Corinthians 6:12). Speaking to others who consumed alcohol, he said, "Be not drunk." He could have said, "Some of you cannot control your drinking. You are a special class of the 'one-drink, one-drunk' kind." But he didn't because there is no such thing.

Interestingly, this same line of reasoning has been used by some Christians to justify the homosexual lifestyle. They create a special category of person—the "constitutionally homosexual person"—of which the Apostle Paul knows nothing. This special person then falls outside of Paul's condemnation of homosexuality, which is seen to be addressed only to heterosexuals who practice homosexuality, not to the "constitutionally homosexual person."

In relation to Step One, much is made of "powerlessness." But the Christian is *not* powerless over sin. It is true that the old nature is powerless against sin and can gain control over our lives (Romans 8:1-11) if we *allow* it to do so. But Christ has freed us from the power of sin and enslavement to the old nature. If we learn to walk in His ways, we can become free of the sinful habits and behaviors of the old nature.

Steps Two and Three say:

2. We came to believe that a Power greater than ourselves could restore us to sanity.

3. We made a decision to turn our lives over to the care of God as we understood Him.

These statements are especially disturbing because they allow and even encourage the addict to view God as a mere concept conformable to the addict's every wish. You can create a God of any sort you want. You can perceive him to be anything you think he is, or ought to be. You can call him anything or anyone you prefer—the choices are practically unlimited. Almost anything goes when it comes to the god of Twelve Stepdom.

Some believe that this fuzzy "God" concept is an advantage, that one ought not to preach Christ at first because of the addict's unstable emotional and spiritual condition. That is, let the addict get sober first; then let him get saved, because God does not require saving faith in order to help the addict stop abusing chemicals.

Morreim[1] sees a "bridge" between Christianity and

Steps 2 and 3, the activity of the Holy Spirit in giving people faith, conversion—from drunkenness to sobriety—and hope for the future. But this is *not* the ministry of the Holy Spirit. Rather, the ministry of the Holy Spirit to the lost is to convict the world of sin, of righteousness, and of judgment to come (John 16:8). The attainment of "sobriety," apart from faith in Christ, is *not* a work of the Holy Spirit.

Step Four sounds very good on the surface; it says:

> 4. We made a searching and fearless moral inventory of ourselves.

Those who advocate the disease model do not consider the behavior that leads to addiction to be immoral. From this point of view, a moral inventory would be absurd. It would be like asking diabetics to make a fearless moral inventory of themselves in relation to their disease.

Even if the alcoholic could perform this moral inventory, on what basis is it to be made? What absolute standard should be used for right and wrong conduct? The moral inventory is usually not moral at all, but rather merely the expression of buried feelings. Morreim says, "[The Twelve Step system] brings people into a continuous program of freedom from the human condition (sin) in their lives . . . Christianity does the same."[2] Without Scripture as the objective standard of right and wrong, however, such determination is made by the way each individual defines the terms.

Step Five is seriously tainted by Step Four. It reads:

5. We admitted to God [whoever or whatever that might be], to ourselves, and to another human being the exact nature of our wrongs.

What is "the exact nature" of the addict's "wrongs"? If the cause of the behavior is biological, "wrongs" is redefined in nonmoral terms. To say, as does the recovery industry, that "the chemical addict is sick, not sinful" is to deny—not admit—the most basic wrong of all. The idea here is that the substance abuser recognizes that even after disclosing the most odious conduct to another person, he will be gratified that the person still accepts him. He may feel greater "self-worth" having unloaded this garbage onto another person.

James 5:16 is frequently used to support the practice of telling your deepest, darkest secrets to a compassionate person. But "admitted" is not the same as "confessed." The end result of confession is forgiveness. But unloading this stuff on another person does not result in forgiveness; only God can forgive sins. Furthermore, the Bible says to seek forgiveness from those against whom you have sinned. Christian Twelve Steppers say that the acceptance of the listener leads the recovering person to sense that he is forgiven and that this is the work of the Holy Spirit.

Some say that in telling their secrets they have "dumped" their guilt and "felt" forgiven. No true forgiveness comes apart from repentance and acceptance of the atoning work of Christ. This is evidence of the movement's inability to distinguish between bad feelings due to guilt and existential moral guilt. The Christian may not feel forgiven after asking God for forgiveness, but feelings have nothing to do with the fact (1 John). The Bible tells us to confess our sins to God and to believe that God has taken them away; feelings will follow.

Morreim says that regeneration is being "grasped by God"—that is, the addict becomes aware of a Higher Power and trusts that Power to keep him sober one day at a time[3] (a totally unbiblical and theologically naive definition of regeneration). He says that the addict's realization that he has been declared "not guilty" because of Christ's death on the cross may not happen when he completes Step Five, but "hopefully that day will come." But what if that day never comes? Those without Christ die eternally lost. What good is a God who gives the addict sufficient grace to become sober but not the grace to save his soul for eternity?

In like manner, Step Six is all but meaningless in light of what the recovery industry tells the addict is responsible for his problem. It says:

6. We were entirely ready to have God remove all of these character defects.

Unfortunately for AA, the disease model makes no provision for character defects. The entire notion of character defects resulting from a disease is an absurdity. One might just as reasonably speak of the character defects of the epileptic. How can one incur a character defect as the result of something over which one has no control?

Step Seven says:

7. We humbly asked Him to remove our shortcomings.

Him who? What shortcomings? Shortcomings such as our inability to run the 100-yard dash in under fourteen seconds? Or shortcomings such as our inability to hold down a job because of our drinking too much too often? Consistent with recovery industry thinking, these are both genetically determined.

Steps Eight and Nine say:

8. We made a list of all persons we had harmed and became willing to make amends to them all.

9. We made direct amends to such people wherever possible, except when to do so would injure them or others.

Steps Eight and Nine are probably the best of the Twelve. The purpose of these two steps is to enable the addict to restore broken relationships. In order to seek forgiveness, he must realize from Step Five that God has forgiven him. But the Bible says that he is only forgiven if he is a Christian. The "big book," *Alcoholics Anonymous,* says, "Our real purpose is to fit ourselves to be of maximum service to God and the people about us."[4] But the Bible teaches that unsaved ones cannot be fit for service to God.

Step Ten, while it may have some practical value, must be considered in light of Step Four. It states:

10. We continued to take personal inventory, and when we were wrong, promptly admitted it.

This is a continuation of the process initiated in Step Four. It is designed to encourage the addict to recognize his "weaknesses" and to admit that he has such defects. Again, with no objective standard by which he might judge right and wrong, he has no reference point with which to evaluate or guide his conduct.

Step Eleven says:

11. We sought through prayer and meditation to improve our conscious contact with God as we understood Him, praying for knowledge of His will for us and the power to carry that out.

From a Biblical perspective, praying to just any power—as if any power might be God—is blasphemous.

Conscious contact with a god that could be any god might lead to contact with the god of this world—Satan. "Knowledge of His will" might be the knowledge of any false god that a Twelve Stepper might create or choose. This is idolatry. God is not constrained to hear the prayers of those outside of Christ. Although it is certainly God's plan for people to be "sober"—in fact, Christians are commanded to be sober—God is under no obligation to answer the prayer for sobriety of a non-Christian. The vital questions are, *whose* will are we talking about, and what is it?

Meditation is essential to Step Eleven. Psalm 119:15, 17 is often quoted in support of the practice. Clearly, though, this psalm refers to meditation on God's Word. The ability to pray is believed by those in the Twelve Step system to be evidence that they have a relationship to God. But apart from Jesus Christ, no man has a relationship to God. Those who believe that a prayer that is not given in the name of Christ improves their "conscious contact with God" are greatly deceived.

Step Twelve states:

12. Having had a spiritual awakening as the result of these steps, we tried to carry this message to alcoholics, and to practice these steps and principles in all our affairs.

This is the most troubling step of all. Twelve Steppers believe that doing the first eleven steps effect a "spiritual awakening" that they should share with others and live out themselves. Romans 12:2 is often quoted in support of this notion. The Apostle Paul was here, however, referring to the rebirth experience, as he was in Colossians 3:9-11. Apart from spiritual regeneration found only in Christ, no spiritual awakening is valid because any other leaves men spiritually *dead*—walking dead men. Any perceived "spiritual awakening" therefore is a deception.

The heart of Step Twelve is carrying the message to other addicts. This is believed to help the Twelve Stepper maintain his "sobriety." The Christianized Compromisers see in the twelfth step a parallel with Christ's Great Commission. This is ludicrous. The Great Commission is the process of spreading the message that Jesus is Lord. Sharing the Twelve Steps with another human being brings no one from darkness into light—only the gospel can do that.

"To practice these steps and principles in all our affairs" demonstrates the pervasive nature of the Twelve Step religious worldview. Morreim says, "AA and the Church are parallel roads, traveling the same direction, covering similar terrain. . . . "[5]

This statement is absolutely false. The Twelve Step system knows nothing of original sin. It allows unregenerate man to ascend to the pinnacle of the universe to declare exactly what kind of God he needs to deal with his drunkenness. The Twelve Step system assumes that the drunkard has the spiritual perception to make a "moral inventory," to know the "exact nature" of his wrongs, to recognize a "spiritual awakening." This is contrary to the Biblical position which teaches that all men apart from Christ are spiritually dead. This spiritual deadness, in fact, has affected man's intellect, will, physical body—his entire being.

The recovery industry's sad track record combined with the Twelve Step's content makes me wonder why anyone—especially a Christian—should take these Twelve Steps. Made out to be a panacea, they do not even seem to be a good placebo. Nevertheless, the homage paid to the Twelve Steps, both by non-Christians and many Christians alike, is nothing less than remarkable.

When I attended a recent Christian Booksellers Association convention, I was amazed at the number of books on display about "recovery" in one form or another. In almost every book I examined, the answer to addiction was the Twelve Steps of AA. While the Twelve Steps were sometimes modified slightly for a Christian audience, and for the particular problem, books advocating the Twelve Steps and the programs built around them were recognized as *the* literature of the enslaved. For example, one program referred to the Twelve Steps as "the most successful approach to recovery ever devised."[6]

Both Bill W. and Dr. Bob were acquainted with the contents of Scripture, but they did not find their answer for the addict in God's Word. Instead, they made the Twelve Steps their savior. The Twelve Steps are imbued with almost divine qualities. In this view, the Twelve Steps provide an application for, insight into, and solution to every addiction problem known to man. Through them you can approach every problem. With them you can understand every problem. By them you can solve every problem.

If this sounds like an overstatement or exaggeration, consider Tim Timmons's book, *Anyone Anonymous*. Timmons is not only mainstream evangelical; he is also middle of the road when it comes to Christians who advocate the use of the Twelve Steps for Christians. He says of the Twelve Steps: "No tool or program has ever been created to equal its effectiveness in aiding the recovery of alcoholics!"[7] Thus, according to Timmons, everyone desiring to help the alcoholic or drug addict recover owes a great debt to AA and the Twelve Steps: "Treatment centers, the world of medicine, the various religious institutions, and virtually every school of therapy must all bow to the powerful dynamics of Alcoholics Anonymous and its Twelve Steps to Recovery."[8]

Why must everyone "bow" to the Twelve Steps? Timmons explains: "The reason is extremely pragmatic: It works! The Twelve Steps are simply profound."[9]

I take serious issue with the notion that AA and the Twelve Steps work. I also fail to see the profundity of which Timmons speaks. Even if the Twelve Steps were profound and viable, that would not make them right.

The fact that something works is no criterion by which to embrace it as being right (cf. Deuteronomy 13:1-5).

Yet, Timmons goes on to say, "Observing the growing interest and the expanded application of the Twelve Steps into all kinds of addiction areas, it became very clear to me that there was no problem area out of their reach."[10] No problem! Surely, this is a bit of hyperbole? Timmons can't really mean that the Twelve Steps are a panacea. *The New Webster's Dictionary of the English Language* defines a panacea thus: "A remedy for all diseases; a solution for any difficulty."

Does Timmons see the Twelve Steps in this way? Judge for yourself. When he says "there was no problem area out of their reach," what does he mean? Timmons explains himself this way: "It's not just for the addictions of our world, but for every conceivable problem man faces!"[11]

If this is not the way to describe a panacea, what would be? So intent on being sure that the reader of his book would get the message, Timmons specifies what some of these nonaddiction problems might be. They are identified as follows:

Personal Problems phobias, depression, low self-esteem, lying, resentment, bitterness, guilt, handicaps (physical, emotional, and mental), abuse.

Relational Problems marital, dating, friendships, conflicts in general, divorce, parental, victimization, loneliness, loss of loved ones.

| Vocational Problems | financial, out of work, dissatisfaction, mistreatment, being fired, bankruptcy[12] |

Just how the Twelve Steps are supposed to help someone who is fired from a job or is blind or lame, Timmons does not say. He does assure us, however, that the Twelve Steps will work for whatever ails you. Thus he says, "Now, I prescribe the Twelve Steps for every problem I face in the counseling room."[13] Not *some* problems, not *most* problems—"*every problem.*"

If the Twelve Steps are for every problem, Timmons should want to prescribe them for himself. And he does, saying: "The real test was when I began to work through the Twelve Steps on my own."[14]

Keep in mind that Timmons is not some "way out on the evangelical fringe" pastor. Rather, he is recognized as a highly successful and respected Christian leader. Nevertheless, he makes an incredible claim: "There has never been a more productive system for personal problem solving than the Twelve Steps of Alcoholics Anonymous. No matter what your problem is, you can solve it by working with these dynamic steps."[15]

Where is the Word of God? Replaced by the Twelve Steps! Please believe me when I say my purpose here is not to pick on Timmons. The reason I have selected quotations from his book is because they are typical of the way many Christian recovery ministries seem to view the Twelve Steps. If I am right about this, we have a very serious problem in the church—and it is not chemical addiction or problems related to drug addiction. Rather it is the loss of all perspective about the true nature of human problems and where the real and ultimate solutions to those problems can be found.

Understandably and predictably, non-Christians will in desperation turn to almost anything they believe might help them out of their plight. But this should not be so for the Christian community. Our unhealthy involvement in and relationship with the world may be the cause of many of our problems in the first place. The world, whether it be in the form of Twelve Stepdom or any other system, does not have the answer. Jesus Christ is the answer.

If your car breaks down, you go to a mechanic. If your body breaks down, you go to a medical doctor. If you are having sin problems, you should turn to the Savior. God's Word does not speak to every issue. It does not tell us how to fix a vacuum cleaner or how to repair a leaky faucet. It does, however, tell us what to do about sin and the human problems sin causes. It provides true insight and real help. As long as we ignore what it says, or water down what it says by mixing in what the ungodly are saying, we will never understand or solve our problems.

Nine

Codependent Cop-out:

Don't Blame Me

In addition to chemical dependency, the recovery industry is reaching out and attempting to treat those suffering from what it calls codependency (or codependence).

Probably almost everyone by now has at least heard of codependency. What it is, exactly, is less clear. According to the recovery industry, codependency is, like alcoholism, a disease. Its primary targets are those who live in close relationship to an addict—a spouse, an addict's children, an addict's parents, etc. Al-Anon, Al-Ateen, even Al-Atot, are all among recovery industry efforts to reach the codependent.

The idea is that the "disease of alcoholism" (or any other addiction) so deeply affects persons who live with an addict that they develop their own disease—codependency—as a result. According to the recovery industry, the codependent is just as powerless to do anything to prevent or cure his disease as the addict. In other words, codependency is simply the disease model of alcoholism extended and applied to those who live with addicts.

The concept of codependency came about as workers in the recovery industry began to observe certain negative behaviors (called "enabling") among those living with alcoholics. Workers considered these behaviors as destructive as the alcoholic's behavior. Codependency advocates say that those who live with an alcoholic are just as dependent on alcohol as the alcoholic himself, because they too are subjected to its destructive effects. Thus, they are "codependent."

Key to understanding the codependency mind-set is the term "enabling." In codependency thinking, those who live with an addict are thought to materially contribute to his addiction by helping to create a favorable environment in which he can indulge. They "enable" the addict to continue his addiction. Enabling includes such behaviors as making excuses for the addict, denying the addiction, covering for the addict, taking responsibility for the addict, and protecting family and friends from the addict's destructive behavior.

It is true that anyone who lives with an addict will have a very difficult time of it. Many of the behaviors labeled "enabling" or "codependent" are simply an attempt to make the best of a bad situation. Sometimes there are no "good choices" when one lives with an addict. Yet, all too often, any attempt to manage a situation caused by an alcoholic is labeled "enabling." Even worse, often those who marry an alcoholic are told they were codependent—usually from growing up in an alcoholic home—even before their marriage. Their codependency, they are told, causes them to recreate the familiar alcoholic environment they grew up in, which in turn brings about their spouse's alcoholism.

But what if it is the *addict* who is responsible? What if his alcoholism (or other addictive behavior) is a decision he makes, not a disease over which he has no control? Much of the enabling and codependency rhetoric disappears (not to mention the multi-billion dollar windfall to the recovery industry).

Another difficulty with the codependency concept is that it tends to extend into every area of human behavior. Codependents, thus, are not limited to people in relation to and adversely affected by chemical dependency. If you are married to or the son or parent of anyone with a serious problem, you are said to be likely to be or to become a codependent. This problem also could be caused by a parent's neglect, abuse, constant criticism, etc. According to this view, almost everyone in a dysfunctional family, for whatever reason that family is dysfunctional, is going to be codependent.

No reasonable person would deny that the spouse, child, parent, etc., of a chemically dependent (or seriously dysfunctional) person may have suffered as a result. Nevertheless, concern about this fact has clearly gotten out of hand. In many cases, the "cure" may be worse than the disease. Disturbingly, the codependency movement has caught fire among Christians, a fact that is especially problematic from the Biblical point of view.

A few years ago the song "This Is Dedicated to the One I Love" topped all the pop charts. At that time everyone understood that to dedicate a song to the one you love was to dedicate it to someone else. When Melody Beattie, author of *Codependent No More,* wrote the first of her several books on codependency, she said: "This book is dedicated to me."[1]

Beattie and others writing on this subject say that the problem with codependents is that they are too concerned about others. They love others too much. They do not love themselves enough, or even at all. "What's a codependent?" asks Lonny Owen. "The answer's easy. They're some of the most loving, caring people I know."[2] According to this view, it's time you made yourself the center of attention. In her second book, *Beyond Codependency,* Beattie explains: "We've started the journey of self-care and self-love."[3]

Tim Timmons expresses the sentiment of the codependency movement (inside and outside the church community) when he says: "The most important person in our lives [is] ourselves."[4]

What about the other-oriented passages of Scripture—for example, chapter 2 of Paul's letter to the Philippians? The Biblical view is that we are to encourage one *another.* We are to edify and build up each *other.* I am to care for you, and you are to care for me. We all need to work on this. Few of our problems result from too much concern for others, and preoccupation with ourselves or our own needs will not solve them. If anything, it will only make emotional and relational matters worse.

Nevertheless, Beattie tells us that *Codependent No More* "has emerged primarily as a book about growing in self-love, and our ability to affirm and nurture ourselves."[5] I am not suggesting that people in general and Christians in particular should hate themselves. This would be unhealthy and unbiblical, although there is a healthy form of self-hatred (cf. Luke 14:26).

Self-centeredness, however, is another matter altogether. The most common justification for this emphasis upon self-love is a misinterpretation of our Lord's command to "Love your neighbor as yourself" (Mark 12:31). Many say that since we are to love our neighbor *as* ourselves, we must first love ourselves. While true, this nevertheless misses the whole point. Obviously, the command to love your neighbor is so that *he* is the *receiver* and that *you* are the *sender* of that love.

If we think of love in practical ways, we see clearly that Jesus is merely paraphrasing the golden rule: "Do unto others as you would have them do unto you" (Luke 6:31). As Paul said, "Each of you should look not only to your own interests, but also to the interests of others" (Philippians 2:4). Notice he did not say you should neglect your interests, only that you should also look to the interests of others.

Looking to our own interests, or loving ourselves, in the sense that our Lord suggests, comes naturally. We are not commanded to do it. It is not something to strive for. As Paul says elsewhere: "No one ever hated his own body, but he feeds and cares for it" (Ephesians 5:29).

It is true that some people, because of mistreatment or abuse in their past, especially their childhood, find it difficult to accept themselves and consequently have a hard time loving others. For these people, the only way they will come to accept themselves and begin to reach out to others is to find their true identity in Christ. For those who have been severely damaged, this may be a long process accompanied by much prayer. This kind of coming into self-acceptance, however, bears slight resemblance to the narcissistic self-love advocated by the codependency movement.

As mentioned earlier, codependents are in one sense believed to be the creation of other dependents. Beattie defines the term: "A codependent person is one who has let another person's behavior affect him or her, and who is obsessed with controlling that person's behavior."[6]

Beattie admits that before she was a codependent and therefore the victim of another "dependent," she was herself chemically dependent. That is, although her codependency was caused by someone else's chemical dependency, as a chemically dependent person, she was creating codependency in others. She says: "As an alco-

holic and addict I stormed through life, helping create
. . . co-dependents."[7]

But it gets even more complicated and confusing.
Chemical dependents create codependents who unwittingly encourage chemical dependency, according to
many in codependency counseling. The codependent
can blame the chemically dependent for creating his
codependency, and the chemically dependent can blame
the codependent for encouraging his chemical dependence. Nan Robertson says of codependents: "They
become enablers . . . no other word is so apt for the person who loves and unknowingly abets the alcoholic."[8]

But it does not stop here. Just as some codependents were first chemically dependent, some chemical
dependents believe they were first codependent.
Timmons says that "alcoholics and addicts noticed they
were codependent and perhaps had been long before
becoming chemically dependent."[9]

In addition to the supposed need of codependents
to make themselves number one, there is another disturbing feature of this movement. This is what I call the
codependency cop-out. No matter what the behavior,
the codependent can explain or rationalize it as a characteristic of codependency.

Beattie explains: "Recovery means dealing with the
entire package of self defeating, compulsive behaviors,
and any other problems that may have emerged. But we
don't deal with these behaviors or problems by thinking
we're bad for having them."[10]

We don't think "we're bad for having them," according to Beattie and others in the codependency movement, because in fact we are not bad for having them. It is not our fault that we are compulsive gamblers, overeaters, fornicators, or workaholics, etc. Indeed, bad behaviors may in this way of thinking be the very best a codependent could do. That is: "We begin to understand that the behaviors we've used were survival tools. We've been coping."[11] For example, if a codependent is hot-headed, mean-spirited, or even violent, he might be using an understandable defense mechanism. The codependent's behaviors, no matter how appalling, "initially are about stopping the pain."[12]

In some cases we are led to believe the pain is so bad that "attacking" others might be the only way codependents have to protect themselves. In *Codependent No More* Beattie seems to excuse such behavior when she says, "They had felt so much hurt that hostility was their only defense against being crushed again."[13]

After all is said and done, Beattie, who admits that the codependent's behaviors are not only bizarre but extreme (and sometimes dangerous), also says: "We've been doing the best we could. We've been protecting ourselves. Some recovery professionals suggest these behaviors may have saved our lives."[14] Sadly, this kind of justification of extreme narcissistic behavior is all too common in the codependency movement.

In summary, the codependency movement not only

suffers from the shortcomings of the broader recovery industry, but also adds some difficulties:

- It buys into the disease model of addiction.
- It tends to label all attempts to deal with difficult situations arising out of living with an addict as "enabling."
- It blames or unfairly implicates victims.
- It identifies character deficits and/or personality problems of those living with addicts as a major contributing factor to addicts' addictions.
- It creates a class of persons ("codependents") whose misconduct is rationalized away as self-protection.

Part 3

Ten

Popular Mistreatment:

Secular Intervention

Unless a chemical addict voluntarily enters a recovery program, the recovery industry recommends intervention. Thus, once someone comes to believe that a spouse, son, or close friend has a serious drinking or drug problem, the recovery industry urges the loved one to prepare to take matters into their own hands. Intervention is that process whereby someone close to the addict confronts the addict with the intention of getting him into treatment. This confrontation is in many instances a prerequisite to treatment. Preparation for the intervention includes the imparting of a great deal of information—indoctrination—about alcohol and drug addiction, much of which the intervener is supposed to communicate to the addict.

The following is a brief summary of what the intervener is likely to be told.

- Chemical addiction (chemical dependency) is a disease.
- As such, it has identifiable symptoms.
- The nature of the disease is that it is:
    primary
    progressive
    chronic
    fatal

By *primary*, indoctrinators mean that the disease is not the symptom of something else (i.e., alcohol or drug abuse), but the source. Not the result but the root. Not the consequence, but the cause of the addict's problem.

To say that this disease is *progressive* is to say that, unless "treated," it will only and always get worse. Accordingly, people with this disease do not get better without treatment.

By *chronic* recovery experts mean that this disease is incurable; it can be treated, but never cured. It is for life.

To say that it is *fatal* means that, unless treated, the addict will die from it. It is only a matter of time.

Obviously, under such indoctrination many potential interveners soon become convinced that treatment is the addict's only hope. After all, without intervention the addict is doomed to self-destruction. Whether from damage directly inflicted by the disease, a car accident while under the influence, or a suicide resulting from depression, etc.—without treatment, the addict will die a premature death. Period. Treatment and only treatment can arrest—not remove—the disease.

In addition, the intervener is told that:

> An alcoholic's recovery is usually connected to his ability to perceive his addiction as a disease.[1]

According to recovery experts, the two most important symptoms of this disease are denial and loss of control. Because it is symptomatic of the disease to deny it, the intervener is told to have patience and to persevere. Opening the eyes of the addict may be very difficult indeed. Rarely does it happen immediately. The denial, however, should be viewed in a strange sort of way as a positive. That is, it is proof or a confirmation of the diagnosis. What more subtle indoctrination could one receive? Concerned family members are told:

> Denial, after all, had been earmarked by Alcoholics Anonymous to be the characteristic symptom and deep core of alcoholism [or drug addiction].[2]

Denial, in turn, is the result of a state of delusion. The intervener is supposed to say something like: "If you did not have an addiction, you could quit. Try to quit. If you can't, then you'll know you are addicted. If you can, no problem—I'm wrong. If, on the other hand, you won't try or you refuse treatment, there will be consequences (I'll take your car—fire you—leave you—etc.)."

Treatment expert Johnson says:

> It will be the task of treatment to make the alcoholic
> [or drug addict] well. It is the task of intervention to
> bring the alcoholic [or drug addict] to treatment.[3]

An intervention allows someone to present the reality of
the situation to the chemically dependent in a manner
the person can accept. This means making the intervention message as palatable as possible. The recovery
industry is convinced that the right and effective way to
intervene is without moralizing or being concerned
about matters of right and wrong.

Stated another way:

> The goal of intervention is to present to the chemi-
> cally dependent data about his chemical dependency
> in a caring and concerned way in order to motivate
> him to obtain . . . help.[4]

This means the intervener must approach the addict in
a way that will not make him feel guilty about what he
has done or is doing:

> The tone of the confrontation should not be judg-
> mental. *The data should show concern; in truth, the facts
> are simply items to demonstrate the legitimacy of the con-
> cern being expressed.*[5]

This process of intervention was popularized by Vernon Johnson in his book *I'll Quit Tomorrow*. Virtually all chemical dependency treatment facilities have since organized procedures for intervention, and some individuals specialize in such methods, giving seminars and writing books.

Although the exact format differs in various localities, the intervention process follows this basic outline:

1. Treatment facility is contacted regarding a person's substance abusing behavior. This contact is made by the spouse who learned of the facility through advertising or by referral—physician, pastor, employer, etc.

2. The spouse then meets with an intervention counselor who identifies those close to the alcohol abuser who are willing to participate in a confrontation. Cost of services information is provided.

3. Training of participants now occurs. They are educated about the "disease" of alcoholism. Data are gathered about the destructive consequences of the abuser's drinking habits. Psychodrama and role playing are often used in preparation for the confrontation. During these sessions certain participants may be "selected out" as inappropriate for the process if they are deemed too emotionally fragile or if they tend to moralize or to be judgmental.

4. The time and date of the intervention is set. It is planned for a time when the abuser is least likely to be under the influence of alcohol such as in the morning.

5. At the intervention *specific* facts about the

abuser's conduct are presented as objectively and unemotionally as possible. Several options are presented (AA attendance, inpatient or outpatient "treatment," quitting on his own), but he must agree to *total abstinence*.

6. If the abuser becomes angry and leaves, at least the "seed" has been planted for dealing with him in the future, even including, if necessary, another intervention session. Recovery experts believe it is rare for the abuser to totally abstain on his own, but he needs to be able to try that option if he chooses. Most likely he will end up in some form of treatment and/or in AA.

MISTREATING ADDICTION

The ultimate success of intervention, of the recovery industry kind, is when the chemical addict submits to treatment. Everything is designed to get the addict into a recovery program. Since the addict is believed to have a lifelong incurable disease, entering a treatment facility, such as a hospital, is only the beginning of never-ending treatment. Much of what the intervener has been told about the disease of alcohol and drug addiction will be repeated over and over to the recipient of treatment.

Consider now, as an example, the case in which a substance abuser has undergone an intervention and has agreed to submit to a recovery program. Upon admission, he will be required to sign an agreement promising to abstain from alcohol and all mood-altering drugs. If he has been coerced into treatment, either by the state or by well-meaning loved ones, he will have no problem signing such a document because he will simply want to get it all over with. If he enters of his own free will, the signing of the agreement may cause him to pause. After all, if he could voluntarily abstain from such drug use, why would he need to be there in the first place?

He will be sequestered in a certain part of the facility where his vital signs will be closely monitored for a period of twenty-four to seventy-two hours or longer in an attempt to spot symptoms of drug withdrawal. After this period, he will be allowed to join the rest of the "patients."

During his hospital stay, he will be introduced to the foundational writings of Twelve Stepdom: *Alcoholics Anonymous*, *Twelve Steps and Twelve Traditions*, and some variety of Twelve Step meditation exercises such as *Twenty-Four Hours a Day* by Hazelden Educational Materials. His daily activities will be rigidly proscribed and will consist of nearly continuous meetings from early in the morning until late at night: group meetings with fellow patients in which he is encouraged to "share," one-on-one sessions with counselors, therapists, physicians, chaplains, etc. He will learn all the current folklore about the "disease" concept of addiction, though it will be presented as scientific fact. All of these indoctrination meetings will be consistent with the Twelve Step worldview.

This brings up a very important point. It may surprise the reader to learn that the goal of treatment is *not* the total abstention from a chemical or from a persistent bad behavioral habit. If that were the goal, recovery programs would be failures because studies have shown that nearly *all* people who complete such programs revert to the behavior in question to at least some degree, even if they eventually become total abstainers. Rather, the goal is to deprogram the patient from a drug-centered lifestyle (a good idea) and to reprogram him with a permanent, lifetime "addict" identity (an exceedingly dangerous idea).

The first two or three weeks of a four-week program concentrate on the addict himself. He is closely observed to see if he is "getting the program." Facts are gathered about him, including his family, his job, what problems in his life need to be addressed. He will be required to write a "first step"—an interpretation of how Step One of the Twelve Steps applies to his life. All the hospital staff with whom he comes in contact will interpret his predicament through a Twelve Step set of "lenses"—no other viewpoint will be entertained.

Enormous pressure is brought to bear upon the substance abuser to accept his new "addict" identity. This pressure comes not only from the treatment facility staff, from which such pressure might well be expected, but often it occurs more cogently from fellow patients, some of whom are undergoing treatment for the second or third time, or perhaps more. If he balks at accepting this identity, he will be ridiculed, cajoled, accused of being in a state of denial. This peer group pressure, working in concert with the constant Twelve Step meetings, seminars, and audio and video presentations designed to indoctrinate him about his "disease" of chemical dependency, makes it very difficult to resist assuming this new identity.

The ambience at the treatment facility is overtly religious—everybody talks about "God," and there is a plethora of religious and devotional materials all around. Plenty of Bibles are there too, though readings from the Bible are generally limited to the Psalms and the Sermon on the Mount, portions of Scripture considered noncontroversial, unoffensive, and nonsectarian. The addict will usually meet one or more times with a chaplain or other "spiritual counselor" because chemical dependency is considered by the movement to be a *spiritual as well as biological problem*. Sound contradictory? That's because it is.

Many eventually "get the program" (incorporate into their being this new identity) though that may not occur until many months after discharge from the treatment facility—only after attending many Twelve Step meetings each week and associating with a new group of Twelve Step friends. "Getting the program" is synonymous with achieving "sobriety," but, according to recovery experts, being "sober" does not mean just total abstinence from chemicals. Rather, it means that one has incorporated a new, permanent "addict" identity, applied the Twelve Step worldview into all areas of his life, and has remained totally abstinent. If the chemical addict "slips" (takes one drink of alcohol or gets drunk once) or relapses (goes on a binge or gets drunk frequently over a short period of time), his sobriety "birth date" is recalculated from the date of his last use of alcohol or other mood-altering substance.

If an addict drops out of the Twelve Step system but remains totally abstinent from chemicals, he is said to be a "dry drunk." He is not sober because sobriety requires the ongoing practice of Twelve Stepping. Some also refer to the state of being a dry drunk as "white knuckle sobriety" and believe that such a person is a veritable walking time bomb, ready to descend with no warning precipitously into orgies of drunken oblivion unless he returns to practicing Twelve Stepdom.

SUMMARY

Treatment, then, involves:
- Re-education or indoctrination.
- Life-time commitment to or association with a support group, which often takes the place of the church.
- Practicing the Twelve Steps in every area of life for the rest of life.

Re-education or indoctrination in the recovery industry means that the one being treated will be taught all about his disease and what he must do to recover from addiction. Since he will learn that, at best, he will always be recovering—never recovered (contrary to 1 Corinthians 6:9-11)—he also learns that he will always need to be in one stage or another of treatment. This recovering stage is called maintenance.

Because the alcohol or drug addict has a special lifetime incurable disease and therefore needs lifelong treatment, he is told he needs the association and support of others who know and understand what his disease is all about. Those who understand his disease and what it takes to remain in recovery are of course others who are themselves in recovery. Alcoholics Anonymous and Narcotics Anonymous are two of the largest such support groups.

Most support groups for alcohol and drug addiction, as well as those for codependents or what are sometimes referred to as co-alcoholics or co-addicts in recovery, practice AA's Twelve Steps. Practicing the Twelve Steps, or what is often referred to as working the Twelve Steps, means the recovering addict must constantly review the Twelve Steps, looking for ways to apply them in all areas of life.

The Twelfth Step of AA requires that the recovering alcohol or drug addict become a kind of evangelist, recruiter, counselor and intervener for the recovery industry. This is a process known as Twelfth Stepping, and it is believed that this reinforces the commitment to maintain recovery.

What you've got here, as you review it carefully, is a pagan substitute for Biblical conversion, teaching, church membership, and witnessing. Twelve Stepdom is a counterfeit of Christianity and competes with it for the souls of men.

Eleven

Road to Restoration:

Biblical Intervention

I f intervention as promoted and practiced by the disease-oriented recovery programs is unbiblical and unacceptable, what can we do for a fellow Christian caught in the clutches of chemical addiction?

We can do a great deal. However, the issue is not intervention versus no intervention. It is rather a Biblically-based intervention versus an unbiblical intervention; appropriate versus inappropriate intervention. Since the recovery industry and its so-called Christ-centered extensions reject the sin label for alcohol and drug addiction, they do not avail themselves of the counsel of God's Word on such matters. But once we come to grip with the fact that Scripture *does* set forth principles that apply to alcohol and drug addiction on every important level—cause, consequence, confrontation, condition—we can then, and only then, apply Biblical solutions to substance abuse.

What we find when we look at alcohol and drug addiction in light of Scripture is a sinner caught up in a sinful addiction. The way in which we view that addiction, including and perhaps especially how it was formed, will go a long way in determining how we intervene and "treat" the one addicted.

What does Scripture say about intervention?

Brethren, if someone is caught in a sin, you who are spiritual should restore him gently. But watch yourself, or you also may be tempted. (Galatians 6:1)

Here we see that Biblical intervention:
● is an obligation.
● should be directed at the one "caught" in a trespass (an excellent description of addiction).
● requires the one intervening to be "spiritual," one who possesses the Spirit who alone can enable one to fulfill this task God's way.
● should be gentle.
● requires the one intervening to take stock of himself, so as to not get in over his head, in trying to help someone else.

Intervention in the Biblical sense is on behalf of both the caught one as well as of the church body which can be, and often is, affected by the unchecked sin of one of its members.

Speaking to the Corinthians, Paul says:

. . . Do you not know that a little leaven leavens the whole lump? Therefore, purge out the old leaven that you may be a new lump, since you are truly unleavened. . . . (1 Corinthians 5:6,7 *Christian Counselor's New Testament*)

In this analogy, leaven represents "malice and wickedness" in an unrepentant church member who must be disciplined. Like leaven in bread, sin tolerated in the church will permeate and contaminate the entire congregation. The one sinning, if need be, must be excommunicated.

If we excommunicated everyone in the church for sinning, the church would of course be empty. It is unconfessed and unrepented sin that Paul addresses here. Excommunication, though at times a necessary measure, should be viewed as the last resort. The goal of discipline is to restore, not to eliminate people. Intervention in a Biblical context is thus interested in reaching substance-abusing Christians in such a manner as to avoid excommunication if possible. The church must, however, be willing to practice excommunication if and when needed. Though a last resort, excommunication is not giving up on the unrepentant sinner; rather, it is the most drastic measure available to the church in order to reach him.

When Paul spoke about leaven being purged, he was not speaking in a vacuum. He had in mind a very immoral man in the church. But at a later time, when the man had come to repentance, in part due to being excommunicated, Paul advised:

> I urge you therefore to reaffirm your love for him. . . .
> If you forgive anyone, I also forgive him. (2
> Corinthians 2:8-10)

Jay Adams, in his *Handbook of Church Discipline,*

identifies five levels of discipline in the church.[1] The first he calls self-discipline.

Level One

Self-discipline (*egkreteia*) is mentioned in Galatians 5:23 as a part of the Spirit's fruit. In Galatians 5:17-23, Paul speaks in terms of two categories or kinds of behavior. The one he calls the works of the flesh and the other the fruit of the Spirit.

The Works of the Flesh	The Fruit of the Spirit
adultery	love
fornication	joy
uncleanness	peace
licentiousness	longsuffering
idolatry	kindness
sorcery	goodness
hatred	faithfulness
contentions	gentleness
jealousies	*self-control*
outbursts of wrath	
selfish ambitions	
dissensions	
envy	
murder	
drunkenness	
"and the like"	

Paul reasons:

Since we live by the Spirit, let us keep in step with the spirit. (Galatians 5:25)

So I say, live by the Spirit, and you will not gratify the desires of the sinful nature. (Galatians 5:16)

Adams explains that:

In 1 Corinthians 9:25 the verbal use of the word refers to self-discipline in athletics: "And everyone who competes in a contest *exercises self-control* in all things."

The idea at the root of the word group has to do with "holding" or "gripping" something. The self-controlled person is one who has a hold or grip on himself, especially on his desires or habitual responses. That is precisely what our reference to the first step in the process of discipline is all about—persons who have such a grip on themselves that they are able to handle problems and relationships in the church and world without the need of help from others.

To be self-controlled does not do away with the strength and wisdom of the Spirit given through His Word. Indeed, *egkrateia* is said to be the fruit of the Spirit (i.e., the result of the Spirit's work) in a believer.[2]

However, as Christians we do not always walk in the Spirit. We do sometimes fulfill the lust of the flesh (as in drunkenness). Thus, self-discipline is not always enough. It is our first and most important line of defense against "leavening the whole lump," but, fortunately, it is not our only defense. When we fail to exercise self-discipline or self-control, Biblical intervention is in order.

Level Two

The second level, according to Adams:

> . . . is the stage where one believer confronts another about what he believes to be the other's sin. The presence of others can certainly complicate the situation.[3]

Adams properly notes that the principle followed in Matthew 18:15 is that a matter must be kept as narrow as the event itself; others are to be called in only reluctantly.[4] Although there are clear guidelines, differences in each situation may often call for a different approach within those guidelines.

> If your brother sins against you, go and show him his fault, just between the two of you. If he listens to you, you have won your brother over. (Matthew 18:15)

Level Three

> But if he will not listen, take one or two others along, so that every matter may be established by the testimony of two or three witnesses. (Matthew 18:16)

Level Four

> If he refuses to listen to them, tell it to the church. . . .
> (Matthew 18:17a)

Level Five

> . . . if he refuses to listen even to the church, treat him
> as you would a pagan or a tax collector. (Matthew
> 18:17b)

Though it is obvious from this text that our Lord is primarily concerned with sins committed by one person against another, the danger of "leaven" in the church gives these instructions a much broader application. Taking these steps not only protects church purity, but church unity as well. Just as important, it provides repeated opportunities for the one in sin to confess and repent. The procedure is to the benefit of everyone involved: the offended, the offender, and the church body of which they are individual members. Intervention in this sense does not guarantee that the offender—the one in sin—will see the sin nor that he will repent of it even if he sees it. It does, however, provide the best possible opportunity for bringing someone back into fellowship with God. We should hope that we never have to go to the last resort of excommunication, but we should be willing and ready to do so if necessary.

Excommunication means that we have no unnecessary association with the offender.

> But now I am writing you that you must not associate with anyone who calls himself a brother but is sexually immoral or greedy, an idolater or a slanderer, a drunkard or a swindler. With such a man do not even eat. (1 Corinthians 5:11)

> Have nothing to do with the fruitless deeds of darkness, but rather expose them. (Ephesians 5:11)

Also, keep in mind that while the benefits of intervention are to everyone, the goal of intervention is restoration of the one overcome by sin. Scripture always assumes the restorability of the sinner. Never does it say that the one "ensnared" by sin cannot help what he does. He may be a "slave" to sin, but Christ can break that bondage. Among Christians, there are no lost causes. The message of intervention, in the Biblical sense, is that the sinner is responsible, both for the sin situation he is presently in, such as an addiction, and for the sinning that brought about that situation.

Intervention for the Christian community should never include the so-called "useful lie." We must always speak the truth in love (Ephesians 4:15). To the extent that we fail to speak the truth, we fail to love. In the long run, trying to make sin seem more palatable by calling it a sickness (for which we are not responsible and from which we need not repent) only impedes real recovery.

If we wish our intervention to be Biblical, we should never do more than what is necessary to bring about restoration. That is, if you alone can work it out with a brother, then do not involve others. If two can take care of it, do not involve the whole church. If the congregation can reach the wayward member, do not resort to excommunication.

Conversely, we should always do whatever is necessary within Biblical guidelines to bring about restoration. That is, if one is unsuccessful, try two or three. If two or three are unsuccessful, then turn to the whole congregation. If the congregation is unsuccessful, excommunicate. Never do more or less than is necessary, and never include more or fewer people than is required.

Now that we have identified some general principles related to Biblical intervention, let's see how they might work in a real-life situation.

Bob and Carol were both Christians and active members of a local evangelical church. Bob was, however, under much pressure at work. On several occasions after retiring, Carol awakened in the late evening to find him missing. On at least two separate evenings she found him in the family room drinking a beer. Carol's father had a serious drinking problem, and so she became very concerned about Bob.

There are a number of things Carol could do at this point. She could call her husband's best friend (also a

Christian) to ask him to talk to Bob. She could call the pastor of her church to provide counseling. If she did either of these things *as a first step* she would have missed an opportunity to intervene in a Biblical manner.

Turning to the pastor or involving a Christian friend may seem harmless and even helpful, but as a *first step* it is unbiblical. It does not give the husband the chance to repent of his sin (if indeed he is sinning) with minimal intervention from others. She may need to bring in the Christian friend or pastor eventually, but at this point that would be premature.

What she should do as a first step is lovingly confront her husband with her concern. If that fails to bring about an adequate explanation or a change (assuming a change is indicated), then she is obliged to take the next step.

Just as some may be tempted to bring in more "troops" than required, others fail to seek enough help when needed. Additional help is indicated when it is clear that step one failed. In some cases that may be immediately. For example, Bob might say, "I am drinking on my own time and in the privacy of my own house. I'm not doing it in front of the kids. I don't drink and drive, get into barroom brawls, or abuse you. I may drink a little more than I should, but I have it under control. What I do therefore is nobody else's business."

If he responds this way, Carol is obliged to take the next step. If she repeatedly takes step one (pestering Bob about his drinking), she will be derelict in her duty.

If however, Bob repents and promises to change (assuming he needs to), a reasonable amount of time should be allowed so that his performance can be compared to his promise. While she should not doubt his sincerity without good reason, neither should she ignore a problem if the repentance is not followed by a change for the better. Bob may be sorry about what he is doing, but he may not sorrow in a godly manner. As Paul says, "Godly sorrow brings repentance . . ." (2 Corinthians 7:10). John the Baptist, who performed the baptism of repentance, called upon those who came to him to be baptized to "produce fruit in keeping with repentance" (Matthew 3:8).

While repentance primarily refers to a change of mind, that change becomes apparent when there is a corresponding behavioral change. If after a reasonable period of time, there is no change, Carol must move on to step two.

When and if step two is required, the additional helper—pastor, Christian friend, family member—is responsible to make sure the charge or accusation is true. One of the reasons the confronter takes one or two more is so that "every matter may be established by the testimony of two or three witnesses" (Matthew 18:16).

Our Lord was calling upon the church to apply a principle of law that is designed to prevent the innocent from being falsely accused and convicted of crimes they did not commit. The *one or two more witnesses* should not enter the picture assuming guilt. Accusations, even from loved ones motivated by love for the accused, are not always true. Failure to heed this principle can lead to disaster.

Step two is also very valuable because if a congregational confrontation with Bob is needed, it would not be just Carol against Bob. Instead, it will be a small group of fellow Christians who care enough for Bob and believe his problem is serious enough to go to all this trouble for him. How church discipline is perceived by everyone involved is extremely important. As Roger Wagner notes:

> It may well be that biblical church discipline is so much neglected in the contemporary Christian world precisely because it is seen as a last resort for "hopeless cases."[5]

However, Biblical discipline should be offered in "hope" of restoration and as a help to that end.

To illustrate how important it is for the helpers to enter the situation with an open mind, suppose it turns out that Bob only has one or two beers a week. Carol, however, painfully remembers that her father started drinking lightly and over a long period of time became a drunk. More significant than what Bob is *doing* is what Carol is afraid it will *lead* to. Bob may need some counsel about foregoing a liberty as a gesture of love and sensitivity. Carol may need to be encouraged to have more trust in her husband. The problem, however, does not require church discipline. Carol's fear that Bob's one or two beers a week may turn into one or two six-packs a night may not be well-founded, but that does not mean that her fear is not real. Total abstinence may be the best and most loving thing Bob can do for Carol.

Those who enter the picture to help can only do so if they exercise the greatest of care. They must keep an open mind as to what the real problem might be. Obviously there is a problem in this scenario, but not as serious as if Bob were actually drinking too much or too often.

If one assumes that all drinking is sinful, then Bob is in sin. However, if moderate drinking is not in and of itself sinful, the problem the helpers face is different from actual alcohol abuse. In light of his own background and experience, Bob may be able in a clear conscience to drink moderately. But he needs to be sensitive to his wife. In light of Carol's experience and background, her fears may be understandable. But she needs to distinguish between a liberty—moderate drinking—and license—abusing alcohol.

Recently a friend who is a Christian talk show host told me about a conversation he had with a caller to his program. It clearly illustrates the need to proceed with caution when exercising church discipline.

Caller: Recently I discovered my pastor was caught up in a sin. I confronted him about it, and he refused to repent. I am now ready to take with me one or two more so that everything can be established. If need be I am prepared to go all the way with this. If he chooses not to repent, I see no alternative but to have him removed as pastor and then excommunicated. But I really love my pastor and believe he is doing a fine job. This is the only area where he is blowing it. I'm calling you to see if you can give me some tips on how to approach him this second time. I want to do all I can to help him.

Friend: How do you know your pastor is in sin?

Caller: I caught him in the act.

Friend: Can you say in what act you caught him and why you think he is unwilling to repent, knowing full well he has been caught?

Caller: He does not repent because he does not believe he has sinned. I walked into a pizza parlor and found him drinking.

Friend: When you say you found him drinking, do you mean you found him drinking a lot, a little, or what? And what was he drinking?

Caller: I do not know how much he was drinking, nor do I care. If I caught someone in a lie or stealing, I would not be concerned how much he lied or stole. I don't even think it is important what a lie is about or what is stolen. Lying is lying, stealing is stealing, drinking is drinking, and sinning is sinning. A little lie is still a lie. Stealing a loaf of bread or stealing a million dollars are both stealing. Drinking a little or drinking a lot is drinking either way. I cannot concern myself with how much he sinned. He sinned and that is all that matters.

Friend: Does your church have a written statement of faith that says moderate drinking is a sin?

Caller: We have the Bible, and so we do not need a statement of faith.

Friend: Where then in the Bible does it say that moderate drinking is a sin?

Caller: Well . . . I guess it doesn't.

I don't mean to suggest that churches should not have a policy against their pastors drinking alcohol, but rather to point out that failure to distinguish between moderate and immoderate drinking only leads to confusion. Those brought into a situation to help had better be on the alert to these issues. Otherwise they may end up hurting more than helping. They must make sure their involvement does not compound the problem. Remember, people are on *firm* Biblical ground only when they can demonstrate drunkenness.

However, what if Bob does have a drinking problem? Suppose it is serious. Maybe he drinks himself to sleep each night. Perhaps he is verbally abusive or is even violent at times with Carol and the kids. Add to all this financial and medical problems. What then?

Obviously it is the intent and teaching of Scripture that discipline should be applied long before it reaches these extreme stages. Nevertheless, no matter how far

Bob's drinking problem has progressed, because it is a sin problem and he is a Christian, the church and everyone involved must try to give him the benefit of Biblically based intervention.

Such a scenario may necessitate other kinds of help as well—medical—for health and safety purposes. But when medical or legal remedies are needed, they should not be viewed as alternatives to church discipline. Medical care when required should always and only be for the medical complications that may accompany chronic alcohol and drug abuse. Bear in mind that alcoholism and drug abuse are moral problems which, by definition, cannot be treated medically. Such treatment is therefore bogus.

If Carol is unwilling to take the first step, someone else in their church must. Legal issues can only be entered into before a court of law *after* excommunication (1 Corinthians 6 forbids taking a Christian brother to court). The person who should intervene is the one who is spiritual (Galatians 6:1)—a Spirit-filled Christian. This is an additional reason not to send people to recovery programs designed and manned by those who do not possess the Spirit.

Again, *never* go to step two if step one succeeds.

And *always* go to step two if step one fails. Were the church a little more faithful and prompt in applying discipline, the more severe steps of congregational confrontation and excommunication would probably only rarely be needed. However, we are so timid and hesitant to exercise this discipline when it is easiest that we are sometimes forced to use it when it is the most difficult. Self-discipline eliminates the need for most one-on-one discipline. One-on-one discipline will eliminate the need for additional help from two or three more, and so on. Remember these principles: Never more than needed; never less than required.

Some, of course, will say, "I tried that discipline stuff and it didn't work." However, church discipline should not be applied simply because we believe it will work. Rather, we must follow it because God commands us to do so. While I prefer to believe that it not only will work, but that it will work best when applied correctly, it should not be viewed as one of many options. It is a Biblical mandate and the only Biblically acceptable way to deal with unrepentant sinners in the church.

Besides, most Christian congregations could not possibly know if church discipline works. How could they know? They have never tried it! No wonder there is so much leaven in the lump.

Until the church repents for not applying discipline when required, many of its members will continue to ignore their sinful behavior. If the problem drinker or drug user does not face up to the sin of his lifestyle, he will never find God's forgiveness for sin. Without forgiveness of sin there can be no real fellowship with God or man. Where church discipline is applied, it is rarely needed. Where it is ignored, the need for it is painfully obvious. May God give us the courage to do what He commands.

Twelve

Maturation vs. Maintenance:

After Biblical Intervention

If a drunkard has really been reached through AA-type intervention, he will believe:

- He was born with a lifelong incurable disease.
- The disease, though incurable, is treatable.
- Post-intervention treatment involves a lifelong maintenance or management program for the disease.

In recovery industry thinking, the "alcoholic" or drug addict is *ever* recovering, *never* recovered. Its advocates would have us believe that alcoholism and drug addiction are to the alcoholic and drug addict what diabetes is to the diabetic. Treatment, including intervention and maintenance and all that these entail (abstinence, Twelve Steps, etc.), is to the recovery industry what insulin and a proper diet are to the diabetic.

Successful intervention of the Biblical kind, however, does not lead to the acceptance of a sickness, but the repudiation of a sin. Intervention by and for Christians should cause the alcoholic to repent and turn from the sin of drunkenness. It also results in forgiveness for that sin and begins the process of restoring the fellowship with God that was interrupted or broken by that sin. Turning from sin and to fellowship with God, is, for the Christian, the way to freedom from the abuse of alcohol or drugs and the addiction that sometimes follows.

While the post-intervention period for the Christian may not always, if ever, be easy, it is maturation in his spiritual life, not the maintenance of an imaginary disease, that should be encouraged and emphasized. Spiritual growth is essential to the Christian delivered from the clutches of alcohol or drug addiction, just as it is to every believer regardless of the choice or degree of sin. The Christian begins the Christian life with spiritual birth (John 3:3) and should continue with spiritual growth (1 Peter 2:2).

When someone believes the gospel, he or she is declared righteous in God's sight—justified by faith (Romans 5:1). From that time on, the Christian should grow out of practicing sin into holiness (sanctification) (2 Timothy 2:21). Without sanctification, maturity is not possible.

Allow me to explain. The greatest single impediment to spiritual growth is sin (Hebrews 12:1). The answer to sin is sanctification, because holiness is, in fact, the antithesis of sin.

Sanctification does not merely mean the absence of sin in the life of the believer, but the presence of holiness. Holiness involves *being* right with God as well as *doing* right for God.

As sanctification excludes sin (which is by definition *against* God), it includes service (which is by definition *for* God). The Christian who is not concerned about sanctification will not grow spiritually. Sanctification is the basis for all spiritual growth. Spiritual growth in turn encourages sanctification—learning more and more to live a holy life. Spiritual growth also requires spiritual nourishment, taking in what God says, as well as spiritual exercise, living out what God requires. To the new Christian, Peter says:

> Like newborn babes, crave pure spiritual milk, so that by it you may grow up in your salvation, now that you have tasted that the Lord is good. (1 Peter 2:2)

Spiritual growth that involves every area of life helps ensure spiritual discernment and stability. As Paul says:

> Then we will no longer be infants, tossed back and forth by the waves, and blown here and there by every wind of teaching and by the cunning and craftiness of men in their deceitful scheming. Instead, speaking the truth in love, we will in all things *grow up* into him [Christ]. . . . (Ephesians 4:14-15)

Spiritual growth will not make anyone invincible. It will, however, make the Christian less vulnerable to negative influences.

> Therefore, dear friends, since you already know this, be on your guard so that you may not be carried away by the error of lawless men and fall from your secure position. But grow in the grace and knowledge of our Lord and Savior Jesus Christ. (2 Peter 3:17-18)

Spiritual growth and sanctification come from choices that the Christian must make each day. Sometimes these choices may be easy. Sometimes they may be difficult. However, we have no way to avoid choosing between light and dark, right and wrong, sin and holiness.

The contrast is between the "works of the flesh," which include "drunkenness" (or drug abuse), and "the fruit of the Spirit," which include "self-control." How do we choose spirituality over carnality? Paul says:

> So I say, live by the Spirit, and you will not gratify the desires of the sinful nature. (Galatians 5:16)

This is a command. We choose whether or not to obey it.

In a discussion of spiritual growth and sanctification, we must not forget the very important concept of discipleship. The word *disciple* in our English Bible is translated from the Greek word *mathatas*. The verb form of this word (*mathono)* means "to learn." Thus a disciple is a learner. Even though all disciples are learners, not all learners are disciples. Christian disciples in the Biblical sense are students of Jesus Christ and are in a special relationship to Him. Christ Himself told His would-be disciples to learn of Him (Matthew 11:29).

Disciples of Jesus Christ must have much more than an academic interest in the Master and His message. As a student of Jesus Christ, the Christian disciple seeks information that leads to transformation. He hears, understands, applies, and then obeys. According to *Vine's Expository Dictionary of the New Testament* the root word *math* in *mathatas* indicates "thought accompanied by endeavor."

The true disciple does not passively listen but actively responds to the teaching and commands of his Lord. That is, he submits to the Lordship of the Savior. He has learned, or is learning, to put Christ above all else (Matthew 10:37-42). He has taken up a cross in anticipation of a crown. He is not following our Lord in blind faith but with an intelligent commitment (2 Peter 1:16). He pays a price in discipleship and in faithfully following the Lord through life. However, while the cost may seem high, the rewards more than compensate. As Paul the apostle put it:

> I consider that our present sufferings are not worth comparing with the glory that will be revealed in us. (Romans 8:18)

The small temporal price is nothing in the light of the great eternal rewards. But even in this life only the committed disciple experiences the "abundant life." The freedom Jesus described was not promised to those who merely come to Him, but to those who continue with Him in discipleship. Remember, it was "to the Jews who had believed him" that Jesus said, "If you hold to my teaching, you are really my disciples. Then you will know the truth, and the truth will set you free" (John 8:31-32).

Discipleship is not an option or elective after the required course of conversion. From the moment immediately following conversion, every Christian should begin traveling down the road of discipleship. As one does, the Master Disciple-maker will always be with him or her (Matthew 28:20). The key verses for us here are John 8:31-32 (quoted above).

While Scripture offers considerable insight and help to the Christian who chooses to turn from sin and return to the Savior, it does not provide a dotted line to follow. Scripture does give us guidelines as well as very clear and specific instruction, but it is not a template for decision making.

Thoughtful consideration should also be given to the Biblical concept of liberty. Christian liberty is the freedom we have in Christ regarding certain things that:

- we are free *not* to do.
- we may not *want* to do.
- we may choose not to do, in love and consideration for someone else who may not be able to do them and

who may be adversely affected if we do them (1 Corinthians 8:9).

● we may choose not to do in some context or with certain company (Galatians 5:13).

That which is a liberty for some may not, in light of a weakness or a personal conviction, be a liberty for others. We should take the weaknesses of others into consideration when we exercise or forego a liberty.

The exercise of liberty with regard to some things, such as drinking alcoholic beverages, is always and without exception to be done in moderation if it is done at all. The liberty to do can never be the liberty to overdo. As Paul said:

> Everything is permissible for me [in context, that which is not, by definition, immoral] but not everything is beneficial. Everything is permissible for me, but I will not be mastered by anything. (1 Corinthians 6:12)

If you drink, you must control your drinking. You may not get drunk. If you use drugs, it must only be in medically supervised and Biblically appropriate ways. Conversely, you must not allow yourself to be controlled by drink or drugs. As everyone knows, even medically prescribed drugs are often abused.

To condemn controlled and moderate drinking, or medically necessary drug use, as such, is legalistic.

Uncontrolled or immoderate drinking or drug use is, however, not liberty but license.

According to Paul:

> It is for freedom that Christ has set us free. Stand firm, then, and do not let yourselves be burdened again by a yoke of slavery. (Galatians 5:1)

While the "yoke of slavery" in this verse refers specifically to legalism (under law), the "yoke of slavery" that comes from being controlled by alcohol or drugs also robs the Christian of his freedom in Christ. Paul warns of this latter kind of enslavement when he says:

> You, my brothers, were called to be free. But do not use your freedom to indulge the sinful nature [i.e., drunkenness]; rather, serve one another in love. (Galatians 5:13)

There is of course a legitimate sense in which the Christian is a slave or servant. As Paul said:

> You have been set free from sin and have become slaves to righteousness. (Romans 6:18)

This kind of slavery, however, is not only consistent *with* but required *for* real freedom. Peter exhorts:

Live as free men, but do not use your freedom as a
cover-up for evil; live as servants of God. (1 Peter
2:16)

Some things we do make living the truly Christian life
impossible. That is why we are commanded not to get
drunk. However, living the Christian life requires more
than the mere absence of sin. As Christians we need
power to be and do as we ought. That is why Paul immediately follows "be not drunk" with "be filled with the
Spirit" (Ephesians 5:18). Christians, like other folk, do
not function well on empty. This is as true spiritually as
it is physically.

So whether you eat or drink or whatever you do, do
it all for the glory of God. (1 Corinthians 10:31)

Often I hear people say something to the effect, "We
can't think that just coming to Christ, praying, reading
our Bible, and attending church regularly is going to
solve all of our problems, especially problems like alcoholism or drug addiction. That's too simplistic."

In reality, coming to Christ, following Christ, and
taking advantage of what is in Christ for us, is far from
simplistic. I do not believe that by simply "praying the
sinner's prayer," all problems will vanish. I do believe,
however, that there has been and will always be infinitely
more help available to the sinner who comes to Christ or

returns to Christ than in all of the recovery industry programs combined.

It is true that some substance abusers come from bad homes. Some have views of God that are patently false. They may see Him as a stern judge or hard taskmaster, and they feel they can never measure up or have His approval. But they keep trying, and their identity is in their inadequate performance rather than in their relationship with God. Many problems from their old sin nature and from emotional or psychological deficits may remain and seem insoluable. When problems such as these are severe, the person may require competent Biblical counseling to overcome the roadblocks to spiritual growth. The salvation Jesus Christ offers includes wholeness, soundness of mind. He is the Great Physician. When He is invited into the places where people are broken and hurting, He brings healing. When people bring their motivations and their "drivenness" to the cross and wait there upon the Lord, He gives insight into the reasons for their behavior. He shows how He Himself meets their needs and fills up their emptiness. We were created to live in union with our Creator, and until we learn to do this—a process—we will ever feel empty and incomplete.

To say Christ is the answer to the problem of alcoholism is not a cliche; it is a fact. Those who label as simplistic a thoroughly Biblical approach to dealing with the problem of substance abuse among Christians woefully underestimate God's power, God's Word, God's love and God's grace. In short, they underestimate God Himself.

However, what about those really "stubborn" sins? "I am not merely tempted to drink too much or misuse drugs," say the "alcoholic" and the "drug addict." "I am driven to do so. I cannot control the urge to misuse substances because the urge and substances control me."

While there are biological consequences to drug habituation, the more prevalent and more serious problem is that as long as people are convinced that they cannot stop doing the things they should not do, they will not stop doing them. It is a problem of false belief. This is, of course, one of the major reasons that teaching the disease concept is so counterproductive. Scripture however, does not recognize "can't help myself" excuses for sin. You do or do not because you will or will not sin. Habitual use, especially habitual use or misuse of potentially addictive substances like alcohol and drugs, can make it extremely difficult to say no. Difficult, but not impossible. Just as habits are made, so they can be broken and replaced. Say "no" enough, and it increasingly becomes easier.

Sinners, such as we all are, never become immune to sinning. However, our strength in the face of sin, our resistance to sin, our resolve not to sin can grow day by day. Some people may always have a more difficult time with certain sins. Those who have a history of alcohol or drug abuse need to be more careful and guarded than others when around alcohol or drugs.

The same can be said for many other kinds of sinning. So-called sex addicts may need, for all I know, to stay away from beaches, *National Geographic*, or even the Sears catalog. They are morally responsible, however, and can, if Scripture is true, refrain from sexual immorality. I do not say this to make light of "sex addiction" or immoral addictions of any kind. I realize that the temptation to sin is all around us, and sometimes seems overwhelming. As powerful as the urge to do wrong is, it is not omnipotent, and Christians are not powerless to overcome it. There is only One who is all-powerful, and that is God. God in turn has given us His Holy Spirit to live and work in us. He has given us the light of His Word to guide us.

The question is, are we taking advantage of the resources we have? Failing to exercise self-control does lead to loss of control. If we have lost control over our lives, we can, however, by God's grace and with His help, take control once again. As the Apostle Peter exhorts, "Make every effort to add to your faith . . . self-control" (2 Peter 1: 5-6).

Thirteen

The Truth and Nothing But:

How to Reach the Unsaved Addict

I can almost hear someone saying, "All you have said up to now sounds fine if you are dealing with a Christian with an alcohol or drug problem. But my husband is not a Christian. He does not believe there is a God, much less does he believe the Bible is God's Word or even true. What, if anything, can I as a Christian, do for him?"

Some of the responsibilities a Christian has to a non-Christian are exactly the same as for another Christian. For example, when Paul tells husbands to love their wives as Christ loved the church (Ephesians 5:25), he is not referring only to Christian wives.

If a non-Christian is working for a Christian employer, at the completion of a day's work, the Christian employer will owe the non-Christian the same amount that he would owe a Christian working at the same pay scale. A Christian employee should work as hard and as well for a non-Christian employer as he would for a Christian employer.

While relationships can be very complex, and responsibilities and roles not always clear, there is one thing that a Christian always owes the non-Christian. The Christian without exception owes the non-Christian the truth. This, I believe, can be thought of in a primary as well as a secondary sense.

THE PRIMARY WAY

The Christian has a commission that translates into his mission for life. It is to *reach* the lost with the love of Jesus Christ—to communicate the good news that Christ died for our sins, rose from the dead, and will someday return; that Christ offers full and free forgiveness to all who will believe in Him and what He has done for them. Every Christian ought to be armed with this message every day. Different kinds of relationships afford different kinds of opportunities and require different amounts of tact. We must walk with wisdom toward those outside the church, but when all is said and done, we should be able to say as did Paul, "I have become all things to all men that by all possible means I might save some" (1 Corinthians 9:22).

We must be flexible, but our aim must be fixed. We must understand that the dynamics of winning a mother to Christ may be different from winning a neighbor. But our goal must remain the same. We must desire to be an instrument of God's saving goodness and grace that our loved ones, friends, neighbors, and anyone else for that matter, may come to know Jesus Christ as their Lord and Savior. A lost loved one, friend, neighbor, may choose to reject the love of Christ, but we must not neglect to share it. This does not mean that our only role and responsibility to a lost person is to reach him with the gospel.

Relationships and the responsibilities that go with them are multifaceted. It should, however, be a primary aim of our lives to win those we can. At this point many will say, "That's fine, but we must get an alcoholic or drug addict free from addiction before he can successfully turn his life over to Christ." While many will become free of addictions before coming to Christ in faith, it is certainly not necessary that it happen in this order. After all, Christ did come "to set the captives free." Jesus Himself said, "So if the Son sets you free, you will be free indeed" (John 8:36). Jesus Christ is, has always been, and will always be the ultimate Liberator.

Chemical addictions are clearly conditions of enslavement, enslavement to chemicals to be sure, but enslavement to sin nonetheless. With some sins, the early stages of enslavement are a simple matter of choice—to do what is wrong. In the latter stages that *same sin* becomes less voluntary and more biologically driven. But in whatever stage one is ensnared, sin still is sin. Paul says, "When you were slaves to sin, you were free from the control of righteousness" (Romans 6:20).

A law of science, I think, illustrates this principle. It says, "A body in motion tends to stay in motion. . . ." Once a locomotive is going in one direction, it naturally tends to continue in that direction. To halt a train with a "full head of steam" takes a strong application of brakes. It can be done and is done every day. But it always and without exception happens only when a person applies the brakes. When a train is brought to a complete stop, it can be made to go in the opposite direction, with the same kind of principle of motion at work. This is the idea in Paul's statement, "But now that you have been set free from sin and have become slaves to God, the benefit you reap leads to holiness, and the result is eternal life" (Romans 6:22).

Just as a train cannot go in two directions at the same time, so a person cannot be simultaneously enslaved to sin and to righteousness. Just as a train that was going in one direction can be halted and taken in the opposite direction, so coming to Christ can turn around one's life. Coming to Christ by faith means to become children of the living God. Paul tells us that, "Therefore, if anyone is in Christ, he is a new creation; the old has gone, the new has come" (2 Corinthians 5:17).

The realization of this change or liberation does not come overnight. In fact, Jesus said, "If you hold to my teaching, you are really my disciples. Then you will know the truth, and the truth will set you free" (John 8:32). And He also said, "I am the truth" (John 14:6).

According to Jesus, His Word is absolutely and perfectly true. Neither sobriety nor "treatment" is prerequisite to the freedom we can have in coming to and continuing with Christ. Thus, if you really want to see your loved ones, friends, or neighbors set free, do whatever you must to introduce them to Him who has brought freedom to countless millions.

THE SECONDARY WAY

The secondary sense in which Christians owe the truth to non-Christians requires an illustration. Suppose a non-Christian came to me for treatment of what he believes is a noncommunicable disease. If it turns out that he actually has a venereal disease, my responsibility is to tell him the truth. This is not only for his sake, but for the sake of those around him who could become infected if he were irresponsible.

Now suppose some of my colleagues said: "Don't tell him he has V.D. There is such social stigma attached to venereal disease. It would be better to tell him he has something that does not involve immorality somewhere along the line. You certainly don't want him or anyone else to know he has a sexually transmitted disease. If you tell him the truth, he is likely to be ostracized and will suffer discrimination."

Sound absurd? It is. But no more so than telling

men and women that the sinful ruin they have made of their lives and the pain they have caused in others is due to a disease. If it is irresponsible and unethical to tell a patient he has one kind of medical condition when he really has another, how much more irresponsible is it to tell someone with a moral problem that he has a medical problem? In the field of medicine, to misdiagnose is to mistreat.

Thus, we can tell the non-Christian—no, we *must* tell the non-Christian—the truth about why he is an addict. One does not have to be a Christian to understand the concept of right and wrong. The chemical addict became such by doing wrong repeatedly and usually over a period of time. If the word *immoral* applies to anything, it applies to alcohol and drug addiction. I'm convinced that anything short of telling the chemical addict that his behavior is immoral and that this immoral behavior has led to a sinful addiction not only compromises ourselves, but cheats him out of the truth.

Some will say, "But you can't talk to nonbelievers about sin or morality. They don't understand or may not be willing to consider such matters."

Can you tell a non-Christian that it is wrong, sinful, or immoral to murder? Can you tell the non-Christian rape is wrong, sinful, or immoral? What about sexually abusing children? Certainly we can and must speak out about sinful and immoral acts when talking to non-Christians. No matter that it is a non-Christian listening, the truth is the truth.

Do we say to a Christian, "If you steal you will go to jail because you know and believe that stealing is wrong, sinful, or immoral" and to the non-Christian, "Since you don't know or believe stealing is wrong, we won't tell you it is wrong or hold you morally or legally accountable if you do steal." This would be absurd, but no more absurd than keeping the truth about chemical addiction from an addict because he is a non-Christian.

Obviously, to approach the non-Christian with a holier-than-thou, self-righteous attitude will be counter-productive. Scripture is abundantly clear that we are *all* sinners, *all* deserving of judgment, and *all* of us have fallen short of God's holy and righteous standards. We should not approach the non-Christian addict to condemn him—he is already under condemnation. We must, however, confront him with the truth.

The truth is that he is an addict because he has been sinning. If we really care about the non-Christian, we will want to alert him to an even more serious consequence of sin than addiction: death. As Paul says, "The wages of sin is death" (Romans 6:23). If it sounds as if I am trying to reduce chemical addiction to a simple matter of sin, it is because I am. Whether he likes it or not, or believes it or not, we owe the non-Christian the truth.

There are two primary reasons I oppose sending the non-Christian to the recovery industry. He will be told his sin is a sickness; he will never be confronted with his real and most basic moral and spiritual problem. And he will more than likely be introduced to the *any god* of Twelve Stepdom, who is, by Biblical criteria, a false god.

These are the very same reasons I oppose utilizing the recovery industry for Christians. Where in Scripture do we find the rationalization, "Don't call this or that what it really is (sin) because someone may be unbelieving or reject the truth?" Nowhere! Where in Scripture do we find Christians telling non-Christians that any god will do? May we find the courage to tell the truth and nothing but the truth.

Janet's Reprise

You will recall that Janet had a fairly serious drinking problem. You will also recall that Janet's husband Dan was approached by his closest friend, Carl, who recommended a recovery program followed by AA membership. From Carl's part onward I would like to rewrite this story. Obviously, we could go back much further to when Dan first recognized his wife was abusing alcohol. Sometimes, however, we have difficulty reaching those to whom we are closest. So let us assume that Carl is the first one to confront the problem. Let us also arm Carl with the information you now know from reading this book.

After Dan unloads, Carl says the following, "Dan, I am very glad you spoke to me. I had no idea this is what was wrong. I think you need to confront Janet with this problem once again. If she is *willing* to change but seems unable to do so, I would recommend she work through this with you and someone in the church who understands the particular dynamics of this sinful behavior. If she has developed a serious chemical addiction, it would be advisable to see a medical doctor to attend to some of the many medical complications that often arise from alcohol abuse.

"But she must realize that abusing alcohol is a matter of choice. It is primarily a spiritual and moral problem. She must recognize her abuse of alcohol as sinful in God's sight, for which there is both forgiveness and freedom. It may be difficult for her at first, but if she resolves to stop abusing alcohol and avails herself of God's grace and whatever encouragement and support you can provide, she will stop.

"Limit the number of people who are involved to no more than needed. Reassure her of God's love and willingness to forgive. Reassure her of God's power to free her from the grip of sin. Help her to understand that Christians can be guilty of almost anything. If this were not so, Scripture would not so frequently warn us about sinful behaviors like drunkenness. After all, if only non-Christians were capable of such sins, all we would need to do is come to Christ. But obviously this is not so; Christians can and do sin in this way. While sin definitely and seriously hinders fellowship with God, Christ does not leave or forsake us. He is ready and willing to forgive. She must confess, repent, and turn from her sin.

"I would also recommend a serious study of discipleship, spiritual growth, and sanctification. If she is unwilling to acknowledge her sin or to turn from it, that of course is another matter. Then you may have to involve others. If she chooses to continue in sin, she is unwittingly inviting church discipline. You will need to be very sensitive and cautious, but you have no other Scriptural choice." What a difference this scenario would make!

Tommy's Reprise

ommy's parents obviously had valid cause for concern. Even if there were no evidence of alcohol or drug use, a drop in grades from A's and B's to C's and D's should disturb any caring parent. But was there any justification for labeling Tommy an addict?

While the one or two beers should be considered unacceptable behavior for a minor and reason for parental intervention, I seriously doubt that alcohol use at this level calls for such drastic measures. Setting aside the issue of treatment effectiveness, it seems to be an attempt to kill a gnat with a sledge hammer.

In Tommy's story, I would like this rewrite to begin just before the director's part. Let's go back to the first time Tommy's parents found out about his weekend drinking. Since Tommy is a minor, there are two separate concerns here. The first, for lack of a better term, I will call the legal concern. Tommy's parents should confront him about breaking the law. One cannot be a lawbreaker without consequences. A society in which people arbitrarily pick and choose which laws they will obey and which laws they will break cannot survive.

If Tommy does not respect the laws of the land as a youth, he may carry this into his adult life with disastrous results. All caring parents are obliged to communicate such concerns to their children.

The other concern, more germane to the purpose of this book, has to do with how much Tommy drinks and in what context. This is what I will call the spiritual and moral concern. While under the laws of our land, he should not drink at all, Tommy's parents should also be concerned with how much he drinks and whether or not he drinks and drives.

Let us suppose that Tommy's parents, instead of going to the youth pastor, went to Tommy first and said something like the following, "Tommy, you know we disapprove of your drinking. You are underage according to the law. As long as it is the law of the land, we cannot allow you to drink. Soon you will be an adult, and you can drink legally if you choose. If you do choose to drink, it should only and always be in moderation. It is especially important that you never get behind the wheel of a car after drinking. If as an adult you decide to use alcohol responsibly, we will respect your choice. If you drink irresponsibly, you will not only be doing wrong according to Scripture, but you will be dishonoring God and doing a great disservice to yourself. We do not believe that having an occasional beer or even experimenting with pot makes you an addict. But underage drinking and using drugs such as pot are wrong.

"We therefore must insist that you wait until you are of legal age to drink. If you do not stop and we find out about it, we will have to take serious measures, such as no driving privileges. Under the circumstances, we will only place you under a two-week restriction. Unless we are given reasons to believe otherwise, we will assume that you are abiding by our wishes."

Jack's Reprise

In this story both Jack and Barbara must utilize Scriptural principles. First of all, Jack needs to understand and be sensitive to Barbara. This means, in light of her background, that drinking alcohol even in moderation should be recognized as a stumbling block. Out of love for his wife, Jack ought to forego or at least greatly limit this liberty. Barbara, on the other hand, needs to learn the difference between use and abuse, between moderate and immoderate, controlled and uncontrolled drinking. She needs to grow in her knowledge and faith so as to know the difference between license and liberty. Imagine how different this story might have been had either of them acted in accordance with Scripture.

≈ ≈ ≈

You may have noticed I did not provide an ending, happy or otherwise, to the rewrites of these stories. The reason is simple. We have no guarantee that a story will end happily. In the real world, even when one party does everything right, the other party or parties can still behave sinfully. While I believe we maximize the opportunities to affect one another in a responsible manner when we act in accordance with Scripture, things do not always turn out the way we would like. Regardless of how things turn out or how people respond to us, we are accountable to God. This means we ought to think, speak, and act in ways that will please Him.

Very few things in life assure us that if one does Y, one can be certain of X. However, God understands your predicament, motivations, and everything about you. He cares for you, Christian, and is able and willing to lead you along the right path. Are you willing, regardless of the consequences, to follow Him? If so, you have no more need for "useful lies."

Notes

CHAPTER TWO *The Diseasing of Christianity: Sin vs. Sickness*

1. Ernest Kurtz, *Not-God: A History of Alcoholics Anonymous* (Center City, MN: Hazelden Educational Materials, 1979), p. 22.
2. *Al-Anon Family Groups* (New York: Al-Anon Family Group Headquarters, 1986), p. 8.
3. Kurtz, *Not-God*, p. 22.

CHAPTER THREE *The Open Secret: Science vs. Sickness*

1. This description of the classic disease concept relies much on Herbert Fingarette, *Heavy Drinking: The Myth of Alcoholism as a Disease* (Berkeley: University of California Press, 1988), pp. 1-2.
2. *Ibid.*
3. These three generations of diseases are set forth in Stanton Peele, *Diseasing of America: Addiction Treatment Out of Control* (Lexington, MA: D. C. Heath, 1989), pp. 5-6.
4. Anderson Spickard, *Dying for a Drink* (Waco, TX: Word Books, 1985), p. 41.
5. Fingarette, *Heavy Drinking*, p. 41.
6. *Ibid.*, p.40.
7. *Ibid.*, notes 5 and 6, p. 34.
8. *Ibid.*, note 20, p. 131.
9. *Ibid.*, p. 128.
10. D. L. Davies, "Normal Drinking in Recovered Alcohol Addicts," *Quarterly Journal of Studies on Alcohol* 23 (1962): 94-104.
11. Mark B. and Linda C. Sobell, *Individualized Behavior Therapy for Alcoholics: Rationale, Procedures, Preliminary Results, and Appendix.* California Mental Health Research Monograph no. 13. California Department of Mental Hygiene, 1972.
12. David J. Armor, J. Michael Polich, and Harriet B. Stambul, *Alcoholism and Treatment* (Santa Monica, CA: The Rand Corporation, 1976).
13. Nick Heather and Ian Robertson, *Controlled Drinking* (London: Methuen, 1981), p. 58.

14. Peele, *Diseasing of America*, p. 81.
15. Nan Robertson, *Getting Better* (New York: Fawcett Crest, 1988), p. 173.
16. Peele, *Diseasing of America*, p. 81.
17. *Al-Anon's Twelve Steps and Twelve Traditions* (New York: Al-Anon Family Group Headquarters, 1981), p. 22.
18. Fingarette, *Heavy Drinking*, p. 72.
19. George E. Vaillant, *The Natural History of Alcoholism* (Cambridge, MA: Harvard University Press, 1983), p. 123.
20. Harold A. Mulford, "Rethinking the Alcohol Problem: A Natural Process Model," *Journal of Drug Issues*, no. 14 (1984): 38.
21. Peele, *Diseasing of America*, p. 62.
22. Goodwin *et al.*, "Alcohol Problems in Adoptees Raised Apart from Alcoholic Biological Parents," *Archives of General Psychiatry* 28: 238-43.
23. Robertson, *Getting Better*, p. 182.
24. K. Blum, E. P. Noble, P. J. Sheridan, *et al.*, "Allelic Association of Human Dopamine D_2 Receptor Gene in Alcoholism," *Journal of the American Medical Association* 263 (1990): 2055-60.
25. Marc A. Schuckit, *Drug and Alcohol Abuse*, 3rd. ed. (New York, London: Plenum Press, 1984), p. 61.
26. *Ibid.*
27. Henri Begleiter, *Alcoholism* 12 (New York, 1986): 488-493, quoted in Schuckit, *Drug and Alcohol Abuse*, p. 69.
28. Gerald G. May, *Addiction and Grace* (San Francisco: Harper and Row, 1988), p. 55.
29. Robertson, *Getting Better*, p. 231.
30. Peele, *Diseasing of America*, pp. 92-95.
31. Robertson, *Getting Better*, pp. 79-80.
32. Peele, *Diseasing of America*, p. 61.
33. *Ibid.*
34. E. Gordis, "Accessible and Affordable Health Care for Alcoholism and Related Problems: Strategy for Cost Containment," *Journal of Studies on Alcohol* 48: 579-85.

CHAPTER FOUR Your Dollars at Work:
The Failure of the Recovery Industry

1. *AA as a Resource for the Medical Profession* (New York: Alcoholics Anonymous World Services, 1982).
2. *Alcoholics Anonymous*, (New York: Alcoholics Anonymous World Services, 1976), p. 58.
3. *Ibid.*

4. *AA as a Resource.*

5. Herbert Fingarette, *Heavy Drinking: The Myth of Alcoholism as a Disease* (Berkeley: University of California Press, 1988), p. 88.

6. Stanton Peele, *Diseasing of America: Addiction Treatment Out of Control* (Lexington, MA: D. C. Heath, 1989), p. 56.

7. F. Baekeland, L. Lundwall, and B. Kissin, "Methods for the Treatment of Chronic Alcoholism: A Critical Appraisal," in *Research Advances in Alcohol and Drug Problems,* vol. 2, eds. R. J. Gibbons *et al.* (Wiley, 1975), p. 306.

8. Peele, *Diseasing of America,* p. 57.

9. *Ibid.,* p. 74.

10. Fingarette, *Heavy Drinking,* p. 89.

11. *Ibid.*

12. *Ibid.*

13. Peele, *Diseasing of America,* p. 73.

14. George Vaillant, *The Natural History of Alcoholism* (Cambridge, MA: Harvard University Press, 1983), p. 284.

15. *Ibid.,* p. 285.

16. Fingarette, *Heavy Drinking,* p. 76.

17. *Ibid.,* pp. 77-78.

CHAPTER FIVE The Legacy of a Useful Lie:
Why the Disease Concept Prevails

1. George Vaillant, *The Natural History of Alcoholism* (Cambridge, MA: Harvard University Press, 1983), p. 20.

2. *Ibid.*

3. Herbert Fingarette, *Heavy Drinking: The Myth of Alcoholism as a Disease* (Berkeley: University of California Press, 1988), p. 23.

4. *Ibid.,* p. 24.

5. *Ibid.,* p. 23.

CHAPTER SIX Christianized Compromise: Addicted to Addiction

1. "Alcoholism and Drug Dependency in the Church," n.d., Overcomers Outreach, La Habra, CA.

2. Alexander C. DeJong, *Help and Hope for the Alcoholic* (Carol Stream, IL: Tyndale House Publishers, 1982), p. 114.

3. *Ibid.,* pp. 114-115.

4. *Ibid.,* p. 22.

5. Anderson Spickard, *Dying for a Drink* (Waco, TX: Word Books, 1985), p. 134.

6. Robert S. McGee, Pat Springle, and Susan Joiner, *Rapha's Twelve-*

Step Program for Overcoming Chemical Dependency (Houston, Dallas: Rapha Publishing/Word, 1990), cover.
7. *Ibid.*, p. 11.
8. *Ibid.*, p. xiv.

CHAPTER SEVEN *The Myth of Christian Origins: Alcoholics Anonymous*

1. *Al-Anon's Twelve Steps and Twelve Traditions* (New York: Al-Anon Family Group Headquarters, 1981), p. ix.
2. *Alcoholics Anonymous* (New York: Alcoholics Anonymous World Services, 1976), p. 46.
3. Bill W., *As Bill Sees It* (New York: Alcoholics Anonymous World Services, 1967), p. 201.
4. *The Clergy Ask About AA* (New York: Alcoholics Anonymous World Services, 1961), p. 9.
5. *Al-Anon's Twelve Steps and Twelve Traditions*, p. ix.
6. *The Clergy Ask About AA*, p. 9.
7. *Came to Believe* (New York: Alcoholics Anonymous World Services, 1973), p. 84.
8. *Al-Anon's Twelve Steps and Twelve Traditions*, p. ix .
9. Ernest Kurtz, *Not-God: A History of Alcoholics Anonymous* (Center City, MN: Hazelden Educational Services, 1979), p. 136.
10. *Ibid.*
11. *Came to Believe*, frontispiece.
12. Igor I. Sikorsky, Jr., *AA's Godparents* (Minneapolis: CompCare Publishers, 1991), p. 13.
13. *Ibid.*
14. *Ibid.*, p. 19.
15. *Ibid.*, p. 1.
16. *Ibid.*, p. 22.
17. *Ibid.*, p. 23.

CHAPTER EIGHT *The Panacea: Twelve Steps to Where?*

1. Dennis C. Morreim, *The Road to Recovery* (Minneapolis: Augsburg, 1990), p. 59.
2. *Ibid.*, p. 68.
3. *Ibid.*, p. 80.
4. *Alcoholics Anonymous* (New York: Alcoholics Anonymous World Services, 1976), p. 77.
5. Morreim, *The Road to Recovery*, p. 132.
6. Robert S. McGee, Pat Springle, and Susan Joiner, *Rapha's Twelve-Step Program for Overcoming Chemical Dependency* (Houston, Dallas: Rapha Publishing/Word, 1990), cover.

7. Tim Timmons, *Anyone Anonymous* (Old Tappan, NJ: Fleming H. Revell, 1990), p. 7.
8. *Ibid.*, p. 7.
9. *Ibid.*
10. *Ibid.*, p. 8.
11. *Ibid.*
12. *Ibid.*
13. *Ibid.*
14. *Ibid.*
15. *Ibid.*, p. 16.

CHAPTER NINE Codependent Cop-out: Don't Blame Me.

1. Melody Beattie, *Codependent No More* (San Francisco: Harper/Hazelden, 1987), dedication page.
2. Melody Beattie, *Beyond Codependency* (San Francisco: Harper/Hazelden, 1989), p. 11.
3. *Ibid.*, p. 8.
4. Tim Timmons, *Anyone Anonymous* (Old Tappan, NJ: Fleming H. Revell, 1990), pp. 23-24.
5. Beattie, *Beyond Codependency*, p. xii.
6. Beattie, *Codependent No More*, p. 31.
7. *Ibid.*, p. 1
8. Nan Robertson, *Getting Better* (New York: Fawcett Crest, 1988), p. 138.
9. Timmons, *Anyone Anonymous*, p. 23.
10. Beattie, *Beyond Codependency*, p. 14.
11. *Ibid.*
12. *Ibid.*
13. Beattie, *Codependent No More*, p. 4.
14. Beattie, *Beyond Codependency*, p. 14

CHAPTER TEN Popular Mistreatment: Secular Intervention

1. Anderson Spickard, *Dying for a Drink* (Waco, TX: Word Books, 1985), p. 134.
2. Ernest Kurtz, *Not-God: A History of Alcoholics Anonymous* (Center City, MN: Hazelden Educational Materials, 1979), p. 193.
3. Vernon E. Johnson, *I'll Quit Tomorrow* (New York: Harper and Row, 1980), p. 65.
4. *Intervention Manual,* The McDonald Center, Scripps Memorial Hospitals, LaJolla, California.
5. Johnson, *I'll Quit Tomorrow*, p. 56.

CHAPTER ELEVEN Road to Restoration: Biblical Intervention

1. Jay Adams, *Handbook of Church Discipline* (Grand Rapids: Zondervan, 1986), p. 29.
2. *Ibid.*, p. 39-40.
3. *Ibid.*, p. 45.
4. *Ibid.*, p. 32.
5. Roger Wagner, "Counseling and Church Discipline," *Journal of Pastoral Practice*, vol. 6, no. 1 (1983): 24.

Bibliography

AA as a Resource for the Medical Profession. New York: Alcoholics Anonymous World Services, 1982.

Al-Anon Family Groups. New York: Al-Anon Family Group Headquarters, 1986.

Al-Anon's Twelve Steps and Twelve Traditions. New York: Al-Anon Family Group Headquarters, 1981.

Alcoholics Anonymous. New York: Alcoholics Anonymous World Services, 1976.

"Alcoholism and Drug Dependency in the Church!" La Habra, CA: Overcomers Outreach, n.d.

Armor, David J., Polich, J. Michael, and Stambul, Harriet B. *Alcoholism and Treatment.* Santa Monica, CA: The Rand Corporation, 1976.

Beattie, Melody. *Beyond Codependency.* San Francisco: Harper/Hazelden, 1989.

———. *Codependent No More.* San Francisco: Harper/Hazelden, 1987.

Begleiter, Henri. *Alcoholism.* 12 (New York, 1986): 488-93.

Blum, K., Noble, E. P., Sheridan, P. J., *et al.* "Allelic Association of Human Dopamine D_2 Receptor Gene in Alcoholism." *Journal of the American Medical Association* 263 (1990): 2055-60.

Came to Believe. New York: Alcoholics Anonymous World Services, 1973.

Davies, D. L. "Normal Drinking in Recovered Alcohol

Addicts." *Quarterly Journal of Studies on Alcohol* 23 (1962): 94-104.

DeJong, Alexander C. *Help and Hope for the Alcoholic.* Wheaton, IL: Tyndale House Publishers, 1982.

Fingarette, Herbert. *Heavy Drinking.* Berkeley: University of California Press, 1988.

Goodwin, *et al.* "Alcohol Problems in Adoptees Raised Apart from Alcoholic Biological Parents." *Archives of General Psychiatry* 28 (1973): 238-43.

Gordis, E. "Accessible and Affordable Health Care for Alcoholism and Related Problems: Strategy for Cost Containment." *Journal of Studies on Alcohol* 48 (1987): 579-85.

Heather, Nick and Robertson, Ian. *Controlled Drinking.* London: Methuen, 1981.

Intervention Manual. LaJolla, CA: The McDonald Center, Scripps Memorial Hospitals, n.d.

Johnson, Vernon E. *I'll Quit Tomorrow.* New York: Harper and Row, 1980.

Kurtz, Ernest. *Not-God: A History of Alcoholics Anonymous.* Center City, MN: Hazelden Educational Materials, 1979.

May, Gerald G. *Addiction and Grace.* San Francisco: Harper and Row, 1988.

McGee, Robert S., Springle, Pat, and Joiner, Susan. *Rapha's Twelve-Step Program for Overcoming Chemical Dependency.* Houston, Dallas: Rapha Publishing/Word, 1990.

Morreim, Dennis C. *The Road to Recovery.* Minneapolis: Augsburg, 1990.

Mulford, H. A. "Rethinking the Alcohol Problem: A Natural Process Model." *Journal of Drug Issues* 14 (1984): 38.

Peele, Stanton. *Diseasing of America.* Lexington, MA: D. C. Heath, 1989.

Robertson, Nan. *Getting Better.* New York: Fawcett Crest, 1988.

Schuckit, Marc A. *Drug and Alcohol Abuse.* 3d ed. New York, London: Plenum Medical Book Co., 1989.

Sikorsky, Igor I., Jr. *AA's Godparents.* Minneapolis: CompCare Publishers, 1990.

Sobell, Mark B. and Linda C. *Individualized Behavior Therapy for Alcoholics: Rationale, Procedures, Preliminary Results, and Appendix.* California Mental Health Research Monograph no. 13. California Department of Mental Hygiene, 1972.

Spickard, Anderson. *Dying for a Drink.* Waco, TX: Word Books, 1985.

The Clergy Ask About AA. New York: Alcoholics Anonymous World Services, 1961.

Timmons, Tim. *Anyone Anonymous.* Old Tappan, NJ: Fleming H. Revell, 1990.

Vaillant, George E. *The Natural History of Alcoholism.* Cambridge, MA: Harvard University Press, 1983.

Wagner, Roger. "Counseling and Church Discipline." *Journal of Pastoral Practice* 6 (1983): 1, 24.

Wilson, Bill. *As Bill Sees It.* New York: Alcoholics Anonymous World Services, 1967.